4 Steps
to bring the
Right Person
into your life
Right Now

4 Steps
to bring the
Right Person
into your life
Right Now

PHILIPPA COURTNEY

Meant2Be Unlimited
San Francisco, California
www.meant2be.com

This book is a work of nonfiction. All the people and stories in this book are real. People's names and some details have been changed to protect their privacy.

This book is not intended as a substitute for professional therapy, and neither the author nor the publisher assumes any liability for damages incurred by following the advice contained or implied in this book.

Meant2Be Unlimited, Inc., San Francisco
First Edition JANUARY 2000
All rights are reserved.

Printed in the United States of America.
09 08 07 06 05 04 03 04 03 02 01 00   5 4 3 2 1

ISBN 1-58639-000-7

Portrait Photography: p. 129, back cover—by Bob Adler
Book Cover and Page Designs by Schwartz Design Group
Copy Fitting and Production by Suzanne Rogers

Publisher's Cataloging-In-Publication Data
  Courtney, Philippa
  4 Steps to bring the Right Person into your life Right Now / Philippa Courtney
  1. Relationships   2. Self-Help   3. Singles
Library of Congress Catalog Card Number: 99-066552

Dedication

They say our personalities are formed before we are six. Mine was set like sweet Jell-O inside my mother's womb as she devoured every romance novel my father could heft back from the bookstore. The saline solution inside her became sweeter with every bodice-ripper she read, and my future more fixed. During my childhood my father worked nights, while I lay in bed transfixed by the romantic tales he made up for me before he left for work. These were what my father called Horlicks' stories, named after the drink that I was supposed to believe was really cocoa.

My prenatal life and early childhood set me on my romantic course. But it was my parents' relationship, their love and commitment for the over fifty-two years they were married, that made me believe in the ability to have a long-term loving partnership.

This book is dedicated to my parents, for the loving example they gave me, and to my husband, Robert, who shows me every day that this kind of love is possible.

Contents

Contents

Dating Tools

Many Thanks To...

Robert, my business partner and husband, for keeping this book on track logically and grammatically. For having the courage to plunge in and become the publisher of this and upcoming books. But most of all, for sharing my passion for this work and encouraging me when I felt "One more rewrite and I will be dead."

Maurice Courtney, my father, for helping me believe I was meant to be a writer. I kept my promise, Dad; this one's for you.

Esther Courtney, my mother, and **Michael Courtney**, my brother, for their encouragement and lifelong belief in me.

Kristin Bole, Laura Walcher, Craig Bouzarth, Louise Berto, and **Luisa Perticucci**, our incomparable book reviewers, for their astute input, which helped me add significant value for the readers of this book.

Mary Kay, Louise, Eli, Joanne, Nancy, Liz, and all our other Meant2Be students and coaching clients, for letting us glimpse into your lives and learn from you.

George Graves, my magical messenger in a bow tie, for opening your heart and sharing your story, so I could see the light at the end of my tunnel.

Bonnie Schwartz and **Amor Fabay Figuracion** of Schwartz Design Group for the book cover, page designs, and much more. Bonnie, we worked together over fifteen years ago, and you are still one of those rare individuals—a creative graphic designer who knows how to meet client and production needs with responsiveness and grace under pressure.

Marilyn Riddle Harper, our editor, who went far beyond the call of duty, addressing structure and grammar at the essence of where it matters, in the heart, as well as the mind, of the reader. As a writer and publisher you understand the doubts experienced by an author. You were wonderfully reassuring. You were all we knew you would be and so much more.

Suzanne Rogers, our production design artist, for copy fitting and transforming my manuscript from merely pages of print into a delight to the reader's eye.

Katherine Prongos, for her eagle eyes and many suggestions that contributed to the readability of the first draft of this book. Your wonderful sense of humor makes you a joy to work with.

Professor Jim Fadiman, a kind man, for taking the time to encourage a total stranger, and help me rekindle the struggling flame of my creativity.

The staff at **Alumnae Resources** in San Francisco, for providing the professional and supportive atmosphere that nurtures the emerging excellence in others. Thanks to you, I had the courage to fly on my own.

And finally, to **most of the men I met and dated**, for driving me to develop this process. May it help each of you find your right one.

Before You Start

What This Book Is and What It Isn't

Many of us think that finding the right person is simply a matter of luck. But I think that being lucky is a matter of being prepared. If that is so, then being lucky means having the knowledge to take advantage of the right time and opportunity when they present themselves. This book will provide you, an intelligent person, with that knowledge, in the form of sound, common sense principles and an absolute minimum of theory. But you'll have to look elsewhere for techniques on kissing or dressing to impress or how to make someone fall for you.

This book is based on the belief that your ideal person is someone who accepts and likes you just the way you are and that you can choose to be around people with whom you feel happy just being yourself. This book is not steeped in psychological theory. You won't be asked to resurrect the past and determine what went wrong and why. We can ruminate from now until forever about why something didn't work, but until we change our thinking and actions, we will keep repeating our painful lessons.

This book doesn't deny that the negative exists. Rather, it focuses on the positive, in order to move you forward so you can shift your thinking and feelings and take the action needed to positively change your life. Interestingly enough, when you do develop a clearer sense of what you want and what will make you happy, you will automatically begin to understand why those other people and relationships didn't work. And surprise, you'll find out that it wasn't your failure or their faults that were to blame. You just weren't right for each other.

This book contains a four-step process through which you are going to discover how to bring people into your life with whom you are comfortable, connected, compatible, and have chemistry. If you are like me, you may have wondered if you are the cause of your flagging social life or failed relationships. But a funny thing happens when you stop seeing yourself as the problem. You step aside and ask the really important questions.

My consulting background taught me to seek answers by taking an inventory of the past. When I inventoried my romantic history, I discovered that I didn't have a clear goal. I did not know what kind of man I really wanted in my life. And if I had defined what I thought was a clear goal, it would have been just a list of attributes, based on what I thought I needed or could have. And I certainly did not have a clear vision. I did not know what my life could be like with the right person. To top it off, I realized that in my personal life I relied heavily on my abilities to relate to people, but without applying all the thinking skills I used in my work life. Does any of this sound familiar to you?

These realizations became the framework for a business-practical, yet heart-centered process by which anyone can bring the right person into their life. Using myself as a guinea pig, I applied a business model to measure my progress and to develop a step-by-step system. This process helped me bring the most compatible potential partners into my life and prepared me to recognize the right one—after a history of choosing the wrong ones. This process can do the same for you.

This business model for personal achievement is based on my experience working with successful business leaders, people who tend to approach life with all cylinders firing. That is why the process in this book is structured to help those of you who are analytical thinkers, as well as those who are more intuitive and feeling based, to use *all* your thinking skills, in order to bring the right person into your life.

I became aware that total-brain thinking was an invaluable asset in business when I was consulting with scientists and engineers in the aerospace, technology, and environmental fields. These were smart people, but I noticed that the ones who depended primarily on their rational/logical mind to solve problems and come up with new approaches were less effective than those who also used their unconscious. Working with these scientists and engineers taught me how to go beyond my own natural creative and intuitive skills. I learned how to use my analytical mind to better plan, assess, and weigh the facts, so that I could make decisions more effectively. It was obvious that we all needed the same skill set to maximize our potential.

Before developing this process, it never occurred to me that the conclusions I came to in my consulting work could also be effective if applied to my personal life, where I made decisions mainly based on instinct and feeling. I used to feel that meeting suitable people could never involve anything logical or systematic. Consequently, my love life always seemed to happen to me. And with all the drama in my life, anyone who knew me then would agree. When my scientist and engineering friends, who had taken an analytical approach to finding a partner, reported that they were equally unsuccessful, I began to think about applying the total-brain model I used in business consulting to my personal life.

It doesn't matter whether you are a more analytical, more emotional, or more intuitive person. What does matter is that you learn how to be all these at different times and in different situations. In your efforts to bring the right person into your life, this will be invaluable. It will mean you can have fun enjoying the great people you meet as a result of this process, while the wiser side of your thinking works behind the scenes to keep you on track.

As you use this process, you will see a noticeable change in the quality and compatibility of your romantic partners. And, as a bonus, learning to harness all your thinking skills will be equally valuable in every area of your life, from your selection of jobs and business partners to your relationships with friends and family members.

Remember: Being lucky is a matter of being prepared, so you can take advantage of the *right time* and opportunity. Now we come to the most important question you need to ask yourself before you read on. *Are you ready to bring the right person into your life?* All the information, support, and tools are here to help you be successful when you are ready. You can choose to read this book, absorb what you learn, and then wait until *your* timing is right before taking action.

I guarantee once you know you are ready, the combination of that certainty and the wisdom of this process will be a powerful catalyst. Your life will change in wonderful ways you only hoped were possible. *You can make it happen.*

Beginnings

How Meant2Be Came to Be

My father used to say that I would know when I met the right one. He was correct: when you listen to your instincts, you are usually right. Unfortunately, our instincts have interference from hormones, romance, the need for companionship, and all the other things that drive us as humans. Small wonder that we wait for someone else or fate to bring the right person into our life. We wait, and since we may not really know what we're waiting for, it takes us a long time to find the right one. And often we end up with the wrong ones while we're waiting.

Up until December 1995, I had not met the right man for me. I was a well-respected, professional businesswoman; people said that I was attractive and I had a great personality. So why wasn't there a special someone in my life? Somewhere in my mid-thirties, after the excitement of my career and exploring life grew tedious, I no longer enjoyed being single. My father's daughter, I always believed you could achieve anything with the right attitude and effort. But when it came to my love life, I was lost in the proverbial forest, bewitched by spells of LUST BLINDNESS and ROMANTIC FANTASIA.

My friends had long since given up on any probability that I would settle down with one person for long, especially at my age. Secretly, I think they were happy with the status quo. After all, I was a constant source of entertainment. All my stories about dates from hell and lust at first sight must have made for interesting kitchen table conversation. So I didn't tell them when the penny finally dropped (a British phrase for when your coin drops into the mechanism that opens the pay toilet), and I realized what I needed to do about my love life. Having heard my previous ideas to purchase a billboard or import someone from England, my friends probably would have put my new realization down to just another wacko scheme to meet the right man. I had tried just about every method you can imagine for meeting the right person, spending literally thousands of dollars on matchmakers, video dating, and special-interest and active singles clubs. I met a lot of men using these methods. Looking back, I can't believe some of the people I dated and how wrong we were for each other. After a while I even started to wonder if there might be something wrong with me.

I read many good self-help books, but I often found their theories complicated and did not relish the idea of reconstructing the painful past through laborious exercises. I knew that I needed a practical, step-by-step process to help me find the right man, a process that would not only give me direction and motivation, but would also reinforce my belief in myself.

The death of my father in 1994 seemed to intensify my need to make positive changes in my life. One day I looked at my professional life, where I felt accomplished, and compared it to my personal life, where I felt such a failure. Suddenly it all became clear: I knew what I needed. I would develop a business-based process for myself. I had no thoughts of sharing the process with anyone else. Little did I know that one day, other people, seeing how this process had worked so wonderfully in my life, would ask me to share it with them and others.

In 1995, having developed a business-practical process for my personal life, I started to put into action the techniques you are now going to discover. My father's death had made me realize I did not want to face another holiday season alone and I placed a romance print ad in a local paper. I had placed ads before, but with the process I had developed I now knew what I wanted. And I believed that I could have it.

People have asked me how I got from feeling like a failure to starting to believe I could have the right person in my life. It didn't happen overnight, but eventually, through a deep spiritual belief that has always sustained me, I found the faith that this could happen, even when I thought I had no more faith to find. My belief is that I am guided and that I already have the answers to what

I am looking for. This time the answers were already in the one area of my life where I always felt confident: my consulting work. Once I started valuing and listening to my wiser self, the answers became clearer.

As I developed this process piece by piece and saw it begin to work in my life, I gained more confidence. By the time I knew I was ready to have the right person in my life, I was able to write an ad so that the kind of men I was seeking were able to recognize themselves in my words. And, I was able to let go of my typical anxiety to make every man I met be Mr. Right. This time it was different. And this time, I had an incredible response to my ad from the type of men who really were just what I wanted.

Six months later, just before the holidays, I met Robert. We were married sixteen months later. He is truly the best present I've ever received. As a part of this process, I had written about Robert before I knew he existed. I became so clear as to what I was looking for that I could precisely describe and sense the kind of person he turned out exactly to be.

For several years, vertically-challenged me struggled alone to trim the vine-covered trellis outside my little house, standing on a wonky ladder. That ladder was a real metaphor for my holding on to bad relationships. I knew I needed a stronger, sturdier one but I held onto that rickety wooden ladder, balancing precariously on one foot, to the amusement of my traditional, married neighbors. They probably had their binoculars out and bets made of when poor, little, lonesome me would topple. Well, I didn't fall off that ladder, but I did take a new approach to pruning my life. And, because of this process, I landed squarely on my feet and in the arms of my leather-jacketed, tall hero who whisked middle-aged, business-suited me off on his big motorcycle.

When Robert and I Met

When Robert and I first spoke on the phone, I wasn't even sure I wanted to meet him. My dance card seemed so full already, and he sounded a bit too East Coast direct for me. He suggested we meet at a special lecture given by an astronaut, with a cocktail party to follow. With a little encouragement from my mother, I said "what the heck" and decided to meet him anyway. I knew he was trouble when I looked up into those mischievous, blue eyes, even if he was dressed conservatively in a navy blue blazer and gray slacks. I was sitting down. Not that it would have made much difference if I were standing up, because I'm the same height standing as he is when he is sitting—he's 6'3". We had discussed basic statistics on the phone, so the height difference wasn't a big surprise to me. Robert, however, later told me that he thought I was too short and too perky. My first impression was that he wasn't my typical lean, artistic, athletic type either. But by the end of the evening, lingering over a late dinner at a vegetarian restaurant, we figured out that we really liked each other and had decided to go out again. That night I wrote in my journal that Robert was nice but not long-term relationship material. Famous last words.

We had been dating for almost a month. Robert was gun-shy from the recent failure of a marriage. True to the process I had developed, I had continued testing the waters, comparing how I felt with Robert to how I felt with the other men I was dating. One evening I had just come home from having dinner with a woman friend when Robert called. Both of us were at the discovery stage and we openly discussed other people we were meeting. He told me he had been out that evening with a woman who fit all the criteria on his "ideal woman" list. I sincerely wished him well. Then he told me that all the time he was with this "ideal woman" he had wished he were with me instead. That was the turning point for both of us.

Like many single people, I used to struggle to say and do the right thing and obtain approval as relationships emerged. As Robert and I got to know each other, however, we constantly remarked about how well we got along. We never had to worry about what to say or how to act. We could just be ourselves. We've come to realize that when you have someone in your life with whom you are truly compatible, this is the way it's supposed to be.

The consistency of the positive feelings Robert and I shared helped me six months later to make the major decision to sell my beloved, little house and move in with him and his fifteen-year-old son. I was tired of living out of a suitcase. When I wasn't away on consulting assignments, I was living between two homes. I was accustomed to living on my own, yet I found it was surprisingly easy to adjust to sharing my life with Robert and his son. All I can say is that I think being with the right person, the person with whom you are truly compatible, makes all the difference in being able to truly share your life with someone. A year after moving in with each other, Robert and I got married and relocated to Northern California.

I'm the kind of person who asks to see the family album when I visit someone's home. Even strangers, sensing my sincere interest in them, have always told me about their romantic concerns. When people everywhere I went learned how I met Robert, and heard the story of the process, they encouraged me to share this special knowledge. By the time we moved to Northern California, I had been informally sharing the process with friends and colleagues for some time.

After the move, I realized that I was burnt-out from my consulting work and ready to reinvent myself. I attended some career transition meetings at Alumnae Resources in San Francisco. One day, I was in a framing shop. The conversation with Mindy, the saleswoman, turned to the process and how I met Robert. Mindy excitedly told me she would love to attend a seminar on the subject if I ever decided to give one. I sought confirmation from a career counselor at Alumnae Resources. She simply asked me what would give me the most pleasure. Without hesitation I answered, "Helping other people bring the right person into their life."

The final piece of the decision puzzle fell into place a few days later, when I was standing on a subway platform looking at a billboard on the other side of the tracks. The billboard said that thousands of people in San Francisco were lonely and it was time to bring them together. It was an advertisement for the romance personals in a newspaper. The message and the timing made me smile. I looked up and mentally thanked God.

This is when I knew it was time to share this wisdom with more than friends. I realized that I had found my calling. Robert, who was at a similar point in his personal growth, shared my desire to make a real contribution. The concept of Meant2Be was born. My career support group at Alumnae Resources gave me the gentle push I needed to get Meant2Be going. One man made me take out a calendar and pick a seminar launch date. Now that the idea was out in the open, I was excited at the prospect of really being able to help people.

As Robert and I faced the turmoil of relocation, a new marriage, and a new career, it became even clearer that the process I had developed had delivered more than I ever thought possible. Even during the worst of times, the foundation of our mutual values and goals and the qualities we initially so liked in each other remain constant. Our finding each other could be construed to have happened for many reasons. But looking at our dismal records for sustaining relationships, it is clear that the quality and depth of our marriage is more than mere coincidence or good luck.

I believe that this process, the Meant2Be Process, prepared me so I could find the person who did not just fill a void in my life, but who filled my soul. If I, a business-smart, 40-ish woman, who had made all the dating mistakes imaginable, could achieve this kind of connection, then I want this for others too. You are going to have someone in your life who is ready to love you, someone who will like you just the way you are, because you are the kind of person they have always wanted to find.

You've Got What It Takes

How the Meant2Be Process Will Work for You

ased on my history of falling in lust or expecting instant intimacy, I can honestly say that if I had met Robert before I developed the Meant2Be Process, I probably would not have recognized that he was the right one. Of course, you don't know that someone is the right one right away. That emerges as you get to know each other. What the Meant2Be Process did for me is help me get in touch with the kind of person with whom I could feel happiest. As I was dating someone, I became aware of the feelings I had when I was with that person, and I could compare that to how I wanted to feel. I learned to understand—and accept—those feelings that became clearer and more consistent as I spent more time with someone. With Robert, the feelings became more positive. When I was with the wrong people my feelings were all over the place and often negative.

Do you meet lots of people through your job or social activities, but still have not found that someone special with whom you want to share a long-term relationship? Or, have you buried yourself safely in your work or your family life? Have you given up on dating because it takes too much time and emotional energy? Has a long-term relationship ended and you find yourself facing the dating scene again, fearful and confused? Are you questioning the current relationship you are in? Are you staying in that relationship and settling because you're not sure there is anything better out there, and if there is, you're not sure you could find it?

As you go through the Meant2Be Process and learn to use the tools needed to achieve your goal, you'll start to believe that finding the right one is possible. Students who have attended our seminars remark how refreshingly positive the Meant2Be Process is. It helps them feel good about themselves again, change their appearance, find better jobs, and generally become more aware of how they can make positive changes in their life.

I do not believe, however, that you need to fix everything about yourself before you can meet the right person. Yes, you may need to clear some emotional baggage to make room for the right person.

> The goal of this process is for you to have
> someone in your life who likes and accepts
> you just the way you are.

And, of course we all want to grow and be the best we can be. But do you need to be "perfect" to have a friend? Of course not. The Meant2Be Process will help you identify and bring into your life the kind of person with whom you can be truly happy. *This means someone who likes you just the way you are—warts and all.*

The techniques you are going to learn will help you discover what makes you feel happy in a relationship. A wise acquaintance of mine, Max, who has been married for thirty years, was asked by his son "How do you know when you are really in love?" He told his son that it is not how you feel about the other person: *it is how you feel about yourself when you are with that person.* In our seminars, I talk about how the Meant2Be Process teaches you how to always be able to answer the most important question:

> How do I feel when I am with this person?
> How does this compare with how I really
> want to feel?

The ability to answer this question provides you with a barometer that registers your AH FACTORS. How do you feel when you step into a Jacuzzi after a hard day's work and sink into the swirling, warm water? That feeling of total relaxation and finally being home is also how you can feel when you are with the right person. This is the AH FACTORS. Robert and I get our AH FACTORS when we're riding his motorcycle with my arms around him, holding him close, as we take the curves of the road together under the open sky. You probably can identify some wonderful AH FACTORS in your own life. Is it when you pet your dog or hold your cat? When you can clearly see and feel the first signs of Spring? Or when you've cranked up the music and have the top down on your convertible? Or when you take that first downhill ski of the season. Or...?

Put "Choose" Back in Your Vocabulary

How are you going to meet enough qualified people so you can choose the right person? Yes, I said *choose!* Unless you are very young, exceptionally good-looking, wealthy, or powerful, you may not have felt that you can attract enough of the right people to choose from. It is time to stop settling and start feeling that you deserve the right person in your life and that you can say no to the people who are wrong for you. It's time to know that you are going to bring the right person into your life. You are going to gain this kind of clarity and confidence through the Meant2Be Process.

A business does not launch a new product without market research. Nor does it expect its targeted customers to buy a new product without first implementing a plan to create awareness. You must create awareness of *you* so the right people know you exist. You are going to discover how to apply some simple, common sense approaches that will help you use dating services and social activities more effectively. By analyzing the potential return on your investment, both financially and emotionally, you'll be able to determine the approaches that will work best for you. Choosing which ways to meet people will depend on your personality, pocketbook, and personal comfort.

And, as you become an educated consumer with a clear sense of what kind of person best suits you, dating services will be able to serve you better. If you are fortunate enough to meet people easily through your work or social contacts and don't need dating services, the Meant2Be Process will help you maximize those opportunities. Either way, you will learn how to spend your time with people who are the best prospects for a happy, meaningful relationship.

Enjoy the Process

You're going to have fun while you work through the Meant2Be Process. But it *is* a process, which means you need to stay on track and follow the process right up through the time you think that you have found that

15

one special person—because that is when you'll be most vulnerable.

Just before I found my right one I was tempted to forget everything I had learned, fall back into my old patterns and settle. It was a true acid test of the Meant2Be Process: would I trust my process and say *no* to what seemed to be a somewhat compatible relationship and consequently open myself up to being alone again? Keep in mind that I was not usually the one who ended relationships. The man I was dating had revealed an aspect of himself that made me realize that I couldn't be truly happy with this kind of person. It was a struggle, but I knew I deserved better. I let the relationship go.

Because I had the courage to say *no* at that time, I was able to open up my life to Robert, whom I ultimately married. I had defined what would make me feel the happiest. I knew that I did not have to settle for less than I deserved. Neither should you.

As you go through the Meant2Be Process, you'll be meeting and spending time with people who come closer to what you are looking for. This is because you'll have a better idea of what it is you want. But you need to meet enough people so you can practice saying *no* to the wrong ones. It's like clearing your old clothes out of the closet so you have room for the new ones that really fit.

In retrospect, the person you eventually choose may surprise you. The right one may be very different from the type of person you usually date. If in the past you have always been attracted to a certain look and personality (this is typecasting), the Meant2Be Process will help you learn how to be more flexible, how to trust your instincts, and how to turn off old programming. My husband and I both had to do that when we first met. Once we got past that, we realized that we had found in each other the person with whom we were the happiest. And yes, the relationship includes all the magic, chemistry, and physical attraction.

While many of the examples in this book are from my personal experience as a 40-ish businesswoman who sought to find a lasting love with a man, the Meant2Be Process can work for anyone, whether you are a man or a woman, whatever your age, and whatever your career, cultural, and religious background.

It doesn't matter how many relationships you have had, or how long it has been since you've dated. This is a new chapter in your life. Turn the page. Turn off all the critical voices. The right person for you is out there. You are now going to learn how to bring that special person into your life.

Step 1: Define the Right Kind of Person for You

How Can I Tell the Difference between Who's Right and Who's Wrong?

W hy is it always easier to identify what we don't want in our lives? Most of us are programmed to easily identify the negatives. It is easy to know what you do not want in someone. You clearly may not want someone who leaves cracker crumbs in the bed or spits olive pits at your mother.

I've learned that what happens in our lives, good and bad, is primarily a result of our own thinking. Remember the saying "Be careful of what you wish for; you may get it"? I believe the same can be said of being careful of what you think about; you may create it. As singles, we have enough negative experiences that our self-confidence is often shaken. Rehashing the past to find out the reasons why relationships failed couldn't motivate me to take the necessary steps to change my life. That's why this Process focuses on the positive.

Step 1: Define the Right Kind of Person for You

How Can I Tell the Difference between Who's Right and Who's Wrong?

Focus on What Makes You the Happiest in a Relationship

We are going to start by determining what you *do* want in someone. Ask yourself this question:

What qualities, traits, and personal style in people allow me to feel happy?

This question can be difficult to answer if you approach it without a framework to focus on the positive. The Meant2Be Process is going to provide you with that framework. Most of us are not conscious of how we feel when we are with different people, much less when we are with the love of our life. When you are with certain people, you just feel good, full of joy, relaxed. And when you are with people who are wrong for you, how do you feel? Anxious? Unworthy? Less than smart?

Am I saying you need someone to make you happy? No.

Happiness comes from within us, not from someone else. But our environment—especially the people in our life—can have a major effect on how much happiness we experience.

Step 1: Define the Right Kind of Person for You

How Can I Tell the Difference between Who's Right and Who's Wrong?

The skills you learn in the Meant2Be Process can be applied to many areas in your life, not just the romantic. You'll learn to become more conscious, more aware, of how you feel and how you want to feel with people. You will go beyond just the facts and impressions you have about someone and start to tune into who they really are. If you have children in the picture, being tuned in can help you sense how your family will feel if the person you are dating becomes part of your lives.

Experts say that getting in touch with how you react to different types of people is a key factor in understanding them and yourself.

Getting in touch with how you react to different people will help enhance your ability to recognize the right person when they come along. As you get to know the people you are dating, you will be able to figure out if they are the right one (or wrong one) faster and more assuredly. In the meantime, you will be protected from falling under the spell of all the things that can get in the way of your better judgement, that is to say LUST BLINDNESS, ROMANTIC FANTASIA, DESPERATE DATING, ticking time clocks, or the advice of well meaning friends and family.

Step 1: Define the Right Kind of Person for You

How Can I Tell the Difference between Who's Right and Who's Wrong?

> Realize that you choose whom you spend your precious time with and how you want to feel when you are with this person. This realization helps you become wiser not only about selecting romantic prospects, but also in choosing friends, business partners, roommates, and others.

Choose to focus on being with people who like you just the way you are—people with whom you can feel your happiest. You will be fueled with the same positive thoughts and feelings you have when you are actually in a wonderful relationship. And, as we all know, positive, assured people are more attractive to all of us. The fact is that your mind does not distinguish between imagination and reality. When you start believing and acting like you have someone special in your life, even if you are not dating, that positive attitude will become contagious.

You may think that asking yourself what makes you the happiest is totally "me" oriented. But keep in mind that when you are sensing how you feel with someone, your antenna will also be picking up how the other person feels about being with you.

Have you ever been on a date and felt like the person across the table from you was delivering a monologue, like you could get up and leave and they would still be talking? How does that make you feel? On the other hand, you know how wonderful it feels to be sitting

Step 1: Define the Right Kind of Person for You

How Can I Tell the Difference between Who's Right and Who's Wrong?

across from someone who listens, asks questions, and seems to really be trying to understand you. Everyone has a basic need to be understood. And when we feel understood we feel connected.

The ability to listen to and understand another person is one of the most powerful tools for establishing rapport.

When working as a consultant, in 1994, I was asked to help a client who had a major communication problem on its hands. The problem was solved when the client team established rapport with the public by learning to sense feelings and communicate understanding.

Los Angeles Department of Water & Power

The Los Angeles Department of Water & Power was ordered by the city council to come to an agreement with a powerful homeowners' group that opposed the siting of a major public facility in a rural canyon. Despite previous mediation attempts, the engineers still felt presenting the facts about the project to the homeowners was like putting their hands into a wasps' nest. Reality to the engineers was a matter of facts. They did not understand that the homeowners' reality was based on perception fueled by emotion. I worked with the engineers to help them learn how to sense the homeowners' feelings and demonstrate an understanding of those

Step 1: Define the Right Kind of Person for You

How Can I Tell the Difference between Who's Right and Who's Wrong?

feelings as they presented the facts. This resulted in both sides being able to openly discuss the issues and resolve them one by one. Not only was costly legal recourse avoided at the time, but both sides were able to let down their guard and have some fun during the meetings.

Think about the people at your work who epitomize effective leadership. Chances are that they are good listeners and that they deal with people effectively because they have taught themselves how to read and sense the people around them. Here is another real-life example of how these skills play out in business.

Andrew Jareki, Cofounder and CEO of Moviephone

After considerable time pondering the pros and cons of being acquired by AOL, Andrew Jareki, Cofounder and CEO of Moviephone, explains how he finally made that major decision for his company's future.

> *"It wasn't until I sat with Bob Pittman, AOL's president and COO, at the premier of You've Got Mail, that the opportunity defined itself...then we had one of those mystical moments when both of us laughed at something; and I thought to myself, "This company [AOL] has a smart guy running it. We could give that company [AOL] the kind of Hollywood presence it needs. There's a love connection here."*
>
> —Fast Times, June 1999.

Step 1: Define the Right Kind of Person for You

How Can I Tell the Difference between Who's Right and Who's Wrong?

Skills like Jareki used to sense how he felt about the AOL's president are something that you can use to benefit your personal life too. Imagine Jareki's story as if it were you meeting someone on a blind date. You are cautious about meeting this person, because it's been a while since you dated and you're unsure whether you want to try again. However, you notice how easily the two of you are talking and laughing together. You realize there is a great deal to admire about this individual, and that you like him or her. By focusing on how you react and feel with the other person you are able to get past your nervousness, relax, and enjoy the moment. After factoring in all these positive feelings, you conclude that it's time to get out and date again, starting now.

Step 1: Define the Right Kind of Person for You

How Can I Tell the Difference between Who's Right and Who's Wrong?

Bring Compatibility and Chemistry Together

There are three key words that will support you as you use the Meant2Be Process. These key words will act as checkpoints to guide you to the right person—and away from the wrong ones. They are the *3-C's:*

Compatibility

The first key word is *compatibility. Compatibility* refers to the qualities, values, goals, and personal style that contribute to your feeling happy when you are with someone. You will learn how to identify this kind of person using the Meant2Be Profile.

When Love Grows in an Absence of Compatibility

Ron is a jovial mechanic and owner of a luxury car repair shop. Divorced, he has three children who live with him part-time. His life is very busy. His girlfriend of three years sees him every other week, when he doesn't have the children. She wants to get married and have a child with Ron. Ron doesn't want to change anything; he definitely doesn't want any more children. He loves his girlfriend, but they spend countless nights breaking up and getting back together again. The difference in their life goals is enormous, but neither wants to face the reality of their incompatibility. They feel trapped and frustrated, yet despair at the idea of leaving each other.

Step 1: Define the Right Kind of Person for You

How Can I Tell the Difference between Who's Right and Who's Wrong?

Connection

The second key word is *connection.* Have you ever been in a foreign country, or moved to a strange town, and not known anybody? Then you bumped into someone from back home, someone who shared the context of your memories. Or have you met someone who shared your passion for something, something that stirred your soul? Remember how that made you feel connected—that you belonged, that you weren't alone? That's what you are looking for when we talk about *connection.*

Comfort

The third key word for you to remember is *comfort.* Have you ever wished that you could have the same easy give-and-take with your romantic dates that you have with your buddies? I used to have a male friend I loved to talk to. We were so accepting of each other that we could just be ourselves. Time with him was so effortless. I wished that I could feel that way with the men I dated, with whom there was excitement but often anxiety. I came to realize that this *comfort,* the feeling of acceptance and relaxation with someone, could coexist with physical attraction.

I once met a man with whom I felt a great *connection.* When he talked about his love of trees and nature and how he understood my closeness to my father, I felt I

27

Step 1: Define the Right Kind of Person for You

How Can I Tell the Difference between Who's Right and Who's Wrong?

had found the one. But while there was *connection* and some *compatibility*, this man had too many walls up. He had recently left a long-term relationship and was still attached to the other person. There was little *comfort* for me. You can only really feel comfortable with someone when they are emotionally available. This goes for your own emotional availability, as well as the emotional availability of the person you are dating. If one or the other is not emotionally available, neither of you will be truly comfortable.

The Urge to Merge

You are probably wondering about that other "C" word—chemistry. Chemistry is probably the single most dominant thought in our mind when we meet someone. This human drive, the *urge-to-merge,* allows us to lower our barriers and risk getting close to people.

Some people define chemistry as mere physical or emotional attraction, but it's far more complex than that. Chemistry has biochemical factors, called pheromones, that scientists are still trying to understand. There are also psychological reasons we are attracted to certain types of people. Chemistry is a concoction of scientific, psychological, and unidentified elements that we do not fully understand, but is something we all want in our romantic relationships. Unfortunately first-date nervousness, preconceptions, and other factors can

Step 1: Define the Right Kind of Person for You

How Can I Tell the Difference between Who's Right and Who's Wrong?

sometimes prevent us from recognizing chemistry when it is in fact there.

So how does chemistry fit into the Meant2Be Process? Physical attraction and romantic feelings are wonderful when they are a balanced part of a full relationship. And you probably know what happens when chemistry becomes the driving force in your efforts to meet the right person. You get LUST BLINDNESS—your hormones are happy, but the rest of you wants more.

I used to believe that chemistry and the *3-C's* were impossible to find in the same person. But the fact is, when you have the *3-C's—compatibility, connection, and comfort*—with someone, your barriers naturally come down, and you want to get closer. The chemistry happens, and it happens at more than just a physical level. Believe me, you'll know it when it's there.

How chemistry fits into your efforts to bring the right person into your life is important, but you don't have to concentrate on it. Think about chemistry as a pot on the stove that simmers away without needing much of your attention. Let chemistry work quietly in the background. Concentrate on the *3-C's* and apply all the other techniques in the Meant2Be Process. Then, you will find a full-bodied, rich relationship, one in which you can be comfortable being yourself, where you have a true life partner and friend—and a relationship that contains plenty of sparks to keep the home fires burning.

Step 1: Define the Right Kind of Person for You

How Can I Tell the Difference between Who's Right and Who's Wrong?

Discover What Makes You Happiest When You Are with the Right Person

If you are like me and have read self-help relationship books, you know they often are full of exercises. Most of us try one or two exercises, lose interest, perhaps read the rest of the book, and go on with our lives. Then when the next relationship doesn't work out we find ourselves back at the bookstore looking for more answers.

There are some tools in this book, like the Meant2Be DateBook and Dating Resource Evaluator, that are here to guide you, but there is only one component in the Meant2Be Process that you really must complete: the Meant2Be Profile. It is the core of the Process. You are not going to compile another list of what your special person has to be like. Rather, you are going to focus on how you want to feel with someone. Remember, getting in touch with how you react to different types of people is a key factor in understanding both them and yourself.

Before you can bring the right person into your life, you need to know what type of person is right for you. The Meant2Be Profile will help you do just that. You are going to start to identify that person by using the Profile to record the qualities, values, goals, and personal style of those people with whom you feel the happiest.

Do you know what makes you happy when you are with the right person? You can find this out by becoming

Step 1: Define the Right Kind of Person for You

How Can I Tell the Difference between Who's Right and Who's Wrong?

aware of when you have felt happiest in relationships with partners, friends, and family, in every major area of your life. The Meant2Be Profile is a tool to help you do this. Then, in Step 2, you will generate an EMOTIONAL-SNAPSHOT of how you want to feel when you are in the right relationship with the right someone. Later, you'll compare your EMOTIONAL-SNAPSHOT of positive feelings generated in your Meant2Be Profile to how you actually feel with the people you are dating. Your EMOTIONAL-SNAPSHOT will bring your special person to life.

Our students find their Meant2Be Profile invaluable in many areas of their lives. One seminar attendee reported using the Profile to enhance her ability to have more meaningful friendships. The Meant2Be Profile also helps people stop seeing themselves as a failure when a partner ends a relationship.

Incompatibility Not Failure

Joe, a student of ours, was delivering a package to an office. He heard about our class while waiting for the receptionist, who was on the phone registering for our seminar. Joe's wife had walked out on him five months previously, after ten years of marriage. When he got home from our seminar he worked on his Profile until after midnight. By the next day he understood why he and his wife were not compatible. He felt tremendous relief now that he knew why the relationship had not worked. Now he

31

Step 1: Define the Right Kind of Person for You

How Can I Tell the Difference between Who's Right and Who's Wrong?

didn't need to see it as his failure. He could stop blaming himself. He also felt more positive, knowing that there was a person out there with whom he was compatible and that he would recognize her when he met her. He felt immediately better about himself, and he noticed that people began responding more positively to him.

You need to complete your entire Meant2Be Profile to help you identify what qualities, values, goals, and style in people make you feel the happiest. We all make our own choices about being happy—people with certain characteristics make these choices easier for us.

Back when astrology was popular, my friends and I used to rush home from first dates to check our astrological charts to make sure the person we had just met was compatible with us. If you are an analytical thinker, there will be a strong temptation for you to use your Profile to assess people the first time you talk to or meet them. Read on, and learn how to use the Profile so it will really work for you.

> You will use your Meant2Be Profile to generate feelings, rather than using it as a template to compare each person you meet against the exact characteristics you have defined.

Step 1: Define the Right Kind of Person for You

How Can I Tell the Difference between Who's Right and Who's Wrong?

The Meant2Be Profile

First, Remember

When I was completing my Profile, I went back and read through my old journals to identify what had made me happiest in past relationships. If, like most people, you don't have journals to help you figure out these things, you may need help triggering your memory.

Ask your friends and family when you seemed happiest in relationships. Did you say anything specific to them that explained your mood at the time? Maybe you entertained more when you were seeing a certain person. This may be a clue to help you realize you've missed that sociability in other, more isolated relationships. Keep in mind that what your friends and family tell you may be colored by their opinions about whom they think you should be dating. Just thank them for their feedback and file their input in the back of your mind. You can decide later if their comments were valid, and how they may apply to how you feel now.

Another way to trigger your memory of how it felt to be with someone with whom you felt happy is to look at old pictures or listen to music you enjoyed at various times in your life. Even if you seem to have only a few good memories of past romances and relationships, there have probably been people in your life with whom you felt happy. Maybe there was a special friendship that triggers thoughts of when you felt your

Step 1: Define the Right Kind of Person for You

How Can I Tell the Difference between Who's Right and Who's Wrong?

best...a time when you felt smarter, wittier, more relaxed, or more complete. If you're having trouble remembering, you can use the examples in the categories of the Meant2Be Profile (on page 52).

As you remember, jot down some notes about the qualities of friends and loves during happy times. Sometimes it is easier to write first about non-romantic friends. Free from the baggage of failed relationships you can write more easily, with warmth and humor.

A word of caution to analytical thinkers: Do not follow your inclination to skip straight to the Meant2Be Profile before you have jotted down some preliminary thoughts. If you do, you may find yourself concentrating on the structure of the categories more than the positive feelings associated with past relationships.

Remember Old Friends as Well

Karen, an accountant, was having problems tuning into positive feelings associated with old relationships. All work, no play, and the fact most of her close friends had left town made quiet Karen feel out of touch with most things positive in her life. I asked her to describe how she felt with Lynne, a close friend she used to know. Karen said that when she was with Lynne she always felt like they would find interesting things to do together. She felt relaxed and accepted, more alive and happy. She realized that this was how she also wanted to feel with the special man she was going to bring into her life.

Step 1: Define the Right Kind of Person for You

How Can I Tell the Difference between Who's Right and Who's Wrong?

Focus on the Positive

Under each of the ten style categories in the Meant2Be Profile (on page 52) you will find a comprehensive list of possible attributes. These suggestions are by no means complete. You may initially think that you would like someone with all the attributes suggested. But please do not simply choose from these suggestions like a wish list. You need to try to identify the positive aspects of people you have known and liked. You have to look back at your own experience and dig below the surface of the suggestions provided. For example, everyone wants someone affectionate, but not everyone wants the same frequency, level, and kind of affection. Use the Meant2Be Profile examples as a guide to add to your notes as you remember other aspects of a relationship in which you felt happy.

Remember, you're completing a Profile of the kind of person you want in your life, based on characteristics in people who make you feel good. *Your focus determines your results.* If you focus on the negative in your Profile, you'll find yourself focusing on negative qualities in the people you meet, and inadvertently attracting exactly the type of person who is not right for you.

Your responses need to be written in the affirmative.

35

Step 1: Define the Right Kind of Person for You

How Can I Tell the Difference between Who's Right and Who's Wrong?

For example, write "eats healthy, well-groomed even when casual, light drinker, and drug-free." Don't write "doesn't eat junk food, doesn't dress sloppily, isn't a heavy drinker, and doesn't do drugs." Focus on the positive!

Identify the Positive People in Your Life

When you remembered what made you feel happiest in relationships, you probably recalled different people. Take a minute and jot down the names of a few people you like and who like you, people with whom you feel relaxed and at your happiest. Under each name, write a few words that describe the type of person they are and how you feel when you are with them. This is the next step to defining which, of all the qualities of a person and a relationship that make you feel happy, are essential in your right one. For example:

Anna

> *Exciting, adventurous, always trying new things.*
> *I'm more outgoing, more alive with her.*

Kevin

> *Caring, easy to be with, someone you can count on.*
> *I feel protected, it's safe to share things about*
> *myself, I feel peaceful with him.*

Step 1: Define the Right Kind of Person for You

How Can I Tell the Difference between Who's Right and Who's Wrong?

You may remember certain special incidents as well as specific people and relationships that remind you what you are looking for in that special someone. One student of ours wished he could have a woman in his life whom he could laugh with, because he kept meeting serious, intense women who were attracted to his intellect. I know exactly what he wanted, because I had a particular blind date that exemplifies this exactly.

Falling for the Wrong One

I met the man at the beach boardwalk. He sat on a high wall at the edge of the sand. After typical pleasantries, I tried to heft myself up on the wall next to him. I over hefted and ended up doing a complete back roll off the wall onto the path behind us. Lying there like a bug on my back with my feet in the air and my skirt over my head, I was engulfed in laughter at the sheer idiocy of my situation. He stood looking down at me, clearly embarrassed and not the least amused at my less than graceful antics. Later, when I was thinking about the kind of man I wanted to meet, I recalled this situation and decided I wanted a man who could laugh at himself even if he fell out of bed at an inopportune moment. I bet you have some incidents in your life that can give you clues about what you are looking for too.

Step 1: Define the Right Kind of Person for You

How Can I Tell the Difference between Who's Right and Who's Wrong?

Compile Your Meant2Be Profile

Completing the Meant2Be Profile isn't something you should rush through. Ideally you want to be in a place where you are comfortable and relaxed—perhaps listening to music that inspires you. I have found that it is easier to save the analysis and editing until after you've made the first pass at completing the entire Profile. You'll probably put it down and then pick it up more than a few times before you feel you've finished it. If you get stuck with a category, go on to another. Later, you'll probably realize you were stuck there for a reason. This is your creation—there are no right or wrong answers. You are not trying to write an essay, so don't worry about the grammar and having a logical flow to your words—it could simply be a list of individual thoughts. Concentrate on the images that come to mind. Write from the heart, not the head. Remember how you feel about your special friends and loved ones. You want the same warmth in the words you use to describe the special person in your Profile as you would use when describing your dearest friends and love ones.

Step 1: Define the Right Kind of Person for You

How Can I Tell the Difference between Who's Right and Who's Wrong?

The Meant2Be Profile Categories

Let's examine the categories in the Profile so you can understand the kinds of questions you need to ask yourself. As we do this, we'll follow the progress of Eric as he completes his Profile and creates his EMOTIONAL-SNAPSHOT.

Eric's Meant2Be Profile

Eric, a stylish man and entrepreneur in the medical device field, has been divorced for about a year and is ready to meet the right woman and start a family in the near future. Eric says that he needs to feel safe with someone so he can demonstrate his romantic, gentle side. He functions well in the analytical mode, and he has had a tendency to focus on what didn't work in his relationships, which resulted in him developing a pattern of negative experiences. Now he wants to get in touch with what makes him feel happy in a relationship.

Physical Style

It's important to distinguish physical style from a person's appearance. We are a very visually stimulated society and it's no wonder we've become preoccupied with how a person looks. When I was placing romance print ads and wrote that I was a redhead, most of the

Step 1: Define the Right Kind of Person for You

How Can I Tell the Difference between Who's Right and Who's Wrong?

responses to my ad were from men who had a thing for redheads. One man who called me after reading my ad interrogated me about the exact color of my hair in sunlight. When I told him it was the color of an Irish Setter he hung up. Clearly he was not a dog lover. I had the same experience with introduction services; they also matched me with men who liked redheads. This wouldn't have been bad if their interest in me had been based on more than my hair color, but it often wasn't. This is what we call "typecasting"—preoccupation with a specific kind of packaging. We all do this to some extent.

Think about the concept of having someone in your life you feel happy with—someone to whom you are attracted. Like the old *Dating Game* TV show, you won't see what the person looks like until after you have determined that they are someone you want to meet.

from Eric's Profile:

Physical Style

- *Dancer's grace*
- *Sense of tasteful glamour and can be natural*
- *Versatile—evening clothes to leather chic*
- *Signature style that stands out from the crowd*
- *Loves perfume and skin creams*

Step 1: Define the Right Kind of Person for You

How Can I Tell the Difference between Who's Right and Who's Wrong?

Emotional Style

This is a very important category; one where you'll want to be sure you've covered all your hot buttons. Experts say that our emotional needs alter over time but our emotional style is unlikely to change. You do not necessarily want someone who has the same emotional style as you; differences can add balance to a relationship.

Your children/no children preference should be addressed in this category because of the emotional significance and impact of that decision. Sue, one of our students, wanted to know how to write in the affirmative that she wanted a man who did not have small children because to her this meant that he wouldn't have enough time for her. As we talked she came to realize that what she really wanted was someone who, if he had small children, could balance his attention between her and his family commitments. I understand her concerns. I didn't plan to meet anyone with teenage kids, but by being open to different possibilities and focusing on the positive, I ended up with a great man who integrated me fully into his life, which includes his super kids, whom I admire and have grown to love.

from Eric's Profile:

Emotional Style
- Playful
- Strong sense of self

41

Step 1: Define the Right Kind of Person for You

How Can I Tell the Difference between Who's Right and Who's Wrong?

- Loves children

- Independent

- Keeps details of our relationship private

Social Style

You are not necessarily looking for someone who has the same social style as you here either. You may, for example, be introverted but feel happiest when you're with someone who gets you out with other people. How do you want your special person to interact with their friends, whether socializing with them on their own or as a couple? Do you like someone who keeps in close contact with his or her friends?

from Eric's Profile:

Social Style

- Let's others be the center of attention

- Great party giver

- Interested in seeing and participating in the latest trends

- Likes trying better restaurants

- Prefers charming B & B's to big hotels

- Loves to travel to exotic places

Step 1: Define the Right Kind of Person for You

How Can I Tell the Difference between Who's Right and Who's Wrong?

Intellectual Style

Let's say that under emotional style you said that you wanted someone very verbally expressive. Now ask yourself about the delivery of that expressiveness. What type of intellectual style do you want in your right one? What makes you most comfortable, being with someone who is articulate and witty, or someone more soft spoken, with a philosophical style?

from Eric's Profile:

Intellectual Style

- *Logical yet expressive*
- *Articulate*
- *Inquiring*
- *Interested in my work, passionate about hers*

Physical Expression

Look at all aspects of each suggestion in the physical expression category. For example, you may feel happiest when you're with someone who is physically demonstrative, but do you want that affection shown everywhere, or are you more comfortable keeping it to private times? You may think you want someone who can fulfill your wildest fantasies, but do you want this kind of relationship on a long-term basis?

Step 1: Define the Right Kind of Person for You

How Can I Tell the Difference between Who's Right and Who's Wrong?

from Eric's Profile:

Physical Expression Style
-Ladylike in public
-Naughty in private
-Likes sensual discovery wrapped in romantic setting
-Bawdy sense of humor
-Loves giving and receiving massages
-Conservative clothes, unbelievable underwear

Communication Style

Communication style is an extension of the intellectual style and, to some extent, the emotional style. They deliberately are kept separate from each other so you can expand your thinking as broadly as possible. When I was doing my Meant2Be Profile I wrote "shares details of his life and make me feel included." I wanted someone who kept in touch when we were apart. Do you feel comfortable with people who express their opinions strongly? Do you have strong opinions? Do you want someone who generally agrees with you or someone who has a different point of view and likes a lively discussion?

Step 1: Define the Right Kind of Person for You

How Can I Tell the Difference between Who's Right and Who's Wrong?

from Eric's Profile:

Communication Style
- *Listens*
- *Expressive*
- *Comfortable with my opinions and sharing hers*
- *Speaks her mind*

Career/Financial Style

Career and finances may not immediately come to mind when you think about what makes you feel happy with someone. But they say most divorces are caused by money problems. If someone is always bouncing checks, is overly tight with money, or is a workaholic and you're not, isn't that going to eventually affect how you feel with that person? So, when you respond to this category, you might write "pays bills on time," "balances personal and career time," or "shares expenses," that is, traits that are important to your happiness. These traits may not be immediately apparent but they will be important to your happiness over time.

Step 1: Define the Right Kind of Person for You

How Can I Tell the Difference between Who's Right and Who's Wrong?

from Eric's Profile:

Career/Financial Style
  - Values long-range planning
  - Is a true partner in regard to
     sharing responsibilities
  - Investment savvy
  - Entrepreneurial

Personal Growth Style

How does a person choose to learn about themselves and their relationships with others? This is their personal growth style. Some people learn about themselves by having friends of the opposite sex or working on their relationship with their family. Others read self-help books or seek professional advice. What style are you most comfortable with? Is your right one someone who is open, wants to discuss life issues with you, and would be amenable to seeing a relationship counselor when needed? Are they someone who shows their growth through their actions but prefers not to discuss it? What is important to your feeling happy and comfortable in a relationship?

46

Step 1: Define the Right Kind of Person for You

How Can I Tell the Difference between Who's Right and Who's Wrong?

from Eric's Profile:

Personal Growth Style

- Likes to read and discuss books on personal growth

- Interested in working on relationship together

- Willing to seek outside advice

Belief (Spiritual) Style

Whatever your beliefs, how the other person thinks about spiritual and religious matters does impact how you will feel in the relationship. I never had alignment in this area with the people I dated before I met my husband. I kept my beliefs to myself or shared just the part that fit in with the other person's beliefs. I found a wonderful *comfort* and reinforcing feeling when I could share my spiritual beliefs and religious practices. Agnostics and atheists may think that having someone who shares their thinking is just as important. Whatever your belief style, it is important that you be honest with yourself about what you want to share, what you are willing to accept, and what you are most comfortable with in other people.

Step 1: Define the Right Kind of Person for You

How Can I Tell the Difference between Who's Right and Who's Wrong?

from Eric's Profile:

Belief (Spiritual) Style
  - Non-practicing Catholic
  - Believes in God and wants to bring our children
    up with an appreciation for our beliefs

Passions

Several years ago I met a man through a romance print ad, someone with whom I seemed to have everything in common. We were both passionate about running, he had two German Shepherds (a breed I adore), we both loved opera and gardening, and he even came from my hometown in England. No, he wasn't my brother, as people at our seminars usually call out. Everything about us fit together perfectly on paper, but when we finally met I felt uncomfortable and on edge around him. All the key aspects that make me feel happy with a person were not there. Of course I didn't understand that at the time; I just felt very disappointed.

Interests are commonly used to superficially match people. Having or acquiring interests in common is good for a relationship, but it is more the style than the specific interests that matters. Robert and I both love the outdoors. He likes it best when he is on a sailboat or his motorcycle. I love being around old trees, and I enjoy being near the ocean. Our mutual style is the

Step 1: Define the Right Kind of Person for You

How Can I Tell the Difference between Who's Right and Who's Wrong?

love of nature and being outdoors. We come together by hiking by the sea or in forests and taking rides on his motorcycle in the country.

> Having interests in common can be an enjoyable enhancement to an existing relationship when the other important parts click. However, common interests are not the most important criteria for *compatibility* when you are evaluating a new relationship.

Limit your responses in this section to your passions— the interests that touch your soul, activities that set your heart racing, pursuits that you really need that special someone to share or at least appreciate with you. What you are looking for is someone whose passions fit your style. Remember that you can always introduce activities and interests to the special person in your life. And you can continue to share your activities and interests with friends.

from Eric's Profile:

Passions

-Psychology and business

-Music — especially my saxophone

Step 1: Define the Right Kind of Person for You

How Can I Tell the Difference between Who's Right and Who's Wrong?

Complete Your Meant2Be Profile

When you think you've finished the first draft of your Meant2Be Profile, put it aside and forget about it for a while. Then, when it is no longer fresh in your mind, come back to it and look at your Profile as an emotionally detached observer. Ask yourself, What surprises me? Which categories have the most words? What are the recurring themes, words, and ideas that appear in different categories? Which categories were the most difficult to complete? How does the input I received from family and friends fit into it? What is missing?

Go through your Profile again. Add, subtract, and edit until it seems on target and clearly identifies the characteristics in people that allow you to feel good when you are with them.

At this point your Meant2Be Profile is just a piece of paper. You've taken characteristics from your experiences with a lot of different people and compiled them in a list. You're probably wondering how you could find all these qualities, or even the majority of them, in one person. Don't concern yourself with all the things you wrote in your Profile. In Step 2 you'll discover how to take your list of attributes from your Meant2Be Profile and bring it to life as you create your EMOTIONAL-SNAPSHOT.

Step 1: Define the Right Kind of Person for You

How Can I Tell the Difference between Who's Right and Who's Wrong?

Who Is Your Right Person?

■ To determine who is compatible with you, it is crucial that you pinpoint exactly what qualities, traits, and personal style in other people contribute to your feeling happy.

■ Focus on how you want to feel when you are with someone. This will also increase your ability to sense how the other person feels about you.

■ Your Meant2Be Profile helps focus you on the positive aspects of people.

■ Your Meant2Be Profile will help you recognize the right person—so you can say no to the wrong ones.

■ Your Meant2Be Profile will fuel your efforts with positive thoughts and feelings—positive thoughts and feelings will make you more attractive in the ways that count.

■ Your Meant2Be Profile will help you discover the direction you need to reach your goal.

■ The Meant2Be Profile is not a template to measure everyone against. It is a tool to help you identify how you want to feel when you are with your right person.

Step 1: Define the Right Kind of Person for You

How Can I Tell the Difference between Who's Right and Who's Wrong?

The Meant2Be Profile

Defining the kind of person you will bring into your life

PHYSICAL STYLE (examples: eats most foods, vegetarian, social drinker, smoke-free, has a sense of color and style, highly-groomed, very healthy, light exerciser, fitness-oriented, high energy level, very relaxed style, fastidious, natural, ???)

EMOTIONAL STYLE (examples: private, sharing, independent, extroverted, introspective, patient, intense, relaxed, faithful, nurturing, wants or has children, happy without children, idealist, realist, generous, ???)

SOCIAL STYLE (examples: people person, private person, sense of humor: slapstick, joke telling, witty, playful; appreciation for "finer" things, appreciation for natural things, lots of friends, a few close friends, likes to be the center of attention, is a listener, likes parties, likes entertaining at home, ???)

Step 1: Define the Right Kind of Person for You

How Can I Tell the Difference between Who's Right and Who's Wrong?

INTELLECTUAL STYLE (examples: artistic, imaginative, scientific, logical, philosophical, inquiring, reader, does crossword puzzles, discusses current topics, debates issues, articulate, ???)

PHYSICAL EXPRESSION STYLE (examples: physically demonstrative in public, physically demonstrative only in private, generous, verbal, directive/initiates, passive, explores new techniques, gives feedback, loves snuggling, ???)

COMMUNICATION STYLE (examples: listens, very expressive, remembers, makes you feel included, keeps in touch, discusses problems, expresses anger in a non-threatening manner, strong opinions, flexible, draws out other people's opinions, ???)

CAREER/FINANCIAL STYLE (examples: systematic (pays bills on schedule), relaxed (pays bills when time permits), good time manager, career focused, personal interest focused, balances personal and professional life, generous, economical, creative, scientific, care giver, service focused, administrative, situational-based ethics, conviction-based ethics, ???)

Step 1: Define the Right Kind of Person for You

How Can I Tell the Difference between Who's Right and Who's Wrong?

PERSONAL GROWTH STYLE (examples: open to counseling, into self-help books, attends seminars, discusses personal growth, will work with partner on relationship skills, seeks advice, works on family relationships, ???)

BELIEF (SPIRITUAL) STYLE (examples: meditates, believes in a higher power, atheist, agnostic, prays, conservative, fundamental, liberal, New Age, Buddhist, Islamic, Jewish, Protestant, lives their beliefs, open to others' beliefs, attends church, studies the Bible, ???)

PASSIONS (examples: a life-goal such as sailing around the world, traveling to the Galapagos, studying art in Italy, animal rescue efforts, ???)

Step 2: Bring Your Special Person to Life

I Know What I Want—
Why Can't I Find Them?

You have completed your Meant2Be Profile. Here it is—paper and ink. Now what? This is a point in the Meant2Be Process where you may be tempted to take a short cut. After all, if you completed your Profile, why do you need to create an EMOTIONAL-SNAPSHOT, *especially if you are the analytical type?*

What Is an EMOTIONAL-SNAPSHOT?

When you look at snapshots of wonderful vacations and special events you recall moments when you felt happy. Imagine a snapshot of you and your right person enjoying a special time together. Instead of visual images, this snapshot contains emotions, feelings you have when you are spending happy times together. This is your EMOTIONAL-SNAPSHOT.

This example may help you understand why you need an EMOTIONAL-SNAPSHOT:

Imagine you are apartment hunting. You've decided you would feel best in a top-floor, corner apartment, less than one mile from public transportation. You view a lot of apartments, and many of them fit your requirements, but none "feel" quite right. Then you happen to see an apartment that clearly doesn't fit all of your requirements, but immediately your gut says "this is the one." It is not a corner apartment, and it is a bit further from transportation than you originally wanted. But there is something about the view from this apartment, the feeling of the living room, and the friendly neighbors, that all together make you feel like you are home. Your laundry list didn't do it: your feelings and instincts were more important.

When Robert and I met, he had a list defining the kind of woman he wanted in his life. I didn't fit his list. Remember I was too short and perky, and scared of the water. But, we liked each other and dated anyway. When we were first dating and still seeing other people, Robert met a woman who fit his wish list. She was the right height, loved sailing, and had a teenage child. But when he was with this woman all he could think about was that he wanted to be with me, not her. This realization for him, and his sharing it with me was the turning point in our emerging relationship.

Why You Need to Create
Your Emotional-Snapshot

It is how we feel about ourselves when we are with someone that is more important than the items on a list. People connect at the emotional level, not the analytical level.

Here's an example of how this works in the business world:

Hewlett-Packard Achieves Objectives

In 1996 I was asked to help one of Hewlett-Packard's internal consulting groups determine what skills, capabilities, and behavioral changes were necessary to increase their management development capabilities.

First, I developed an assessment (a profiling tool) in the form of a written questionnaire for each member of the group to complete. As is often the case with assessments, there was resistance to fully answering each of the questions. Next, I conducted personal interviews, during which I sensed each person's emotional responses as we discussed the questions and their answers.

The written responses identified only the symptoms. They indicated a gap in skills and capabilities. If that was the problem, then training was the answer.

But the personal interviews showed the employees in fact had the required skills. However, some did not believe in their ability to apply them, while others felt that the corporate culture would not reward them if they used these skills.

Because the findings and recommendations rang true to people's feelings the report I presented was accepted wholeheartedly.

It was the emotional pictures, and not the written facts, that clearly pointed out the blocks to behavioral change that stood in the way of achieving corporate objectives.

You have to go beyond the list of facts in your Meant2Be Profile. Before you can bring your right one to life you need to create an EMOTIONAL-SNAPSHOT based on the feelings your Profile evokes.

Create Your EMOTIONAL-SNAPSHOT

Ready? Get out your Meant2Be Profile. Reread each of the ten style categories. What are the recurring themes, words, or ideas? What are the central themes, the most important thoughts, the words that evoke the most emotion? Use these themes and ideas to write a few sentences or paragraphs that generate strong feelings—an emotional picture of the type of person who is right for you. When you can imagine how it feels to have this person in your life, and you feel excited about this, then you have your EMOTIONAL-SNAPSHOT .

Getting from Your Profile to Your EMOTIONAL-SNAPSHOT

If your Profile describes someone who is easy going (Emotional Style), who likes to listen (Communications Style), and who is laid-back and relaxed with friends known since high school (Social Style), then you may get a picture in your mind of someone who reminds you of an old-fashioned, understated, movie hero, someone naturally good-natured and comfortable just being with people, without having to prove himself, someone you can count on. When you can imagine having this person in your life you feel at peace. There is a lack of tension when you are together. Life is simple. You don't need excitement and drama; you have each other and a few good friends. The two of you can sit together on your porch swing with your dog and feel connected without the need for words.

Let's look at the EMOTIONAL-SNAPSHOT Eric created from his Meant2Be Profile. Remember that Eric is a strongly analytical individual, but he recognized that he liked a woman who balanced, rather than matched, this quality in him. He also knew that he tended to be a more introspective person and that he felt attracted to more extroverted women, but not someone too gregarious either. After analyzing what he'd written in his Profile, Eric took out his saxophone and lost himself in his music, stopping to jot down thoughts as they came to him. He kept zeroing in on his special woman's style and presence, the fact that she was playful and self-confident enough to encourage his successes, which, being himself entrepreneurial, he thought was very important. After several iterations, Eric came up with this EMOTIONAL-SNAPSHOT.

Eric's EMOTIONAL-SNAPSHOT

When she walks into a room you can feel her presence, without her having to do anything. Her clothes and the way she moves all seem at ease yet distinctive. But she makes it plain that she's with me. She puts her arm around me and smiles. As soon as we met, we could be playful with each other, teasing, being silly. She makes me feel confident and at ease. With her I feel ready to take on the world. I'm proud of her accomplishments. She is proud of mine.

You know you have the right EMOTIONAL-SNAPSHOT when the thoughts from your Profile generate powerful feelings and images. Eric definitely felt this. When he talked about meeting this woman, his face lit up.

How to Know Your EMOTIONAL-SNAPSHOT Is on Target

One of our students, Janet, a single mother, reports that when she had finished compiling her Profile she had a very clear emotional image of the kind of man she was seeking. Shortly after creating her EMOTIONAL-SNAPSHOT, she received a call from a man whom she had dated many years ago. She had not thought of him or heard from him in a long time. He was happily married, but for some reason he had been thinking about her. As they talked about old times, he recalled how wonderful they had felt around each other, and how much fun it was just doing nothing special together, like grocery shopping, or cooking. What Janet found more amazing than the fact that this old friend had called her, was that he used the exact words she had written in her EMOTIONAL-SNAPSHOT: "It doesn't matter what we do when we're together, it feels wonderful." She felt this call was a confirmation, a

> validation that she was on the right track, that her
> EMOTIONAL-SNAPSHOT was on target. She knew she
> was getting close to meeting her special man.

Don't worry about what happens to all the rest of the stuff you wrote in your Meant2Be Profile. Your unconscious mind has already filed away all this data for you. Once you meet that special person, you will be amazed to find that not only do they fit your EMOTIONAL-SNAPSHOT, but as you will come to learn, also many of the other things you indicated in your Profile. This happens with many of our seminar attendees, just as it did to me. When I met Robert, he fit my EMOTIONAL-SNAPSHOT. Later I found he fit 98% of the Profile I had written, a Profile I had deliberately forgotten about. So, when you are finally finished with your Profile, when you have created your EMOTIONAL-SNAPSHOT and it makes you feel strongly about your right one, put your Profile aside so that you will not be tempted to use it as a template with everyone you meet.

Believe Your Right One Exists

Start with the proposition that you *believe* the kind of person you described in your EMOTIONAL-SNAPSHOT *can and does exist.*

Now take this belief to the next step. *Know* that you are going to bring this kind of person into your life.

What if you have no positive role models to help you believe that someone like you, whatever your age, appearance, or economic circumstances, can have that special person in your life? You may have done a good job of convincing yourself that it's unlikely, if not impossible, that it's going to happen.

How do you get from self-doubt to knowing that this is possible? Ask yourself, What is the worst thing that can happen? If you think opening yourself up to believing and then suffering disappointment is the worst thing that could happen, then think again. The worst thing that can happen is that you limit the potential for joy in your life by being unwilling to take a risk.

If you are still hesitant, try this simple exercise:

You Are a Risk-Taker Who Succeeds

In ten-year increments, representing the ages in your life, write when you made a significant change in your life, changes that resulted in a positive outcome. You'll be pleasantly surprised how many risks you have taken that have resulted in great things happening in your life.

Our student Janet says she gets to the point of knowing she is going to meet her right man by listening for signals from God that she's doing the right things—like the call from her old boyfriend after she developed her EMOTIONAL-SNAPSHOT. If you are still grappling with getting to knowing that you can bring that special person into your life, sometimes all you can do is take a leap of faith. Try acting like you believe and know it to be true. You will start noticing little things happening, clues that you are on the right track. Soon you will really believe that you can bring the right person into your life.

> *How different our lives are when we really know what*
> *is deeply important to us, and keeping that picture in*
> *mind, we manage ourselves each day to be and to do*
> *what really matters most.*
> —Stephen Covey, 7 Habits of Highly Effective People

Our students tell us that as soon as they start working on the Meant2Be Process, even before they have completed Step 1, new people start showing up in their lives. The fact that you made the decision to buy this book and find out how to bring the right person into your life was the start of things changing positively for you. Your unconscious mind already knew you were ready.

Everyone Can Find Their Right One

My friend Suzanne is a perfect example of someone who had many doubts and fears about ever finding the right partner. A 42-year-old, petite powerhouse, she fenced, drove her sports car with precision, and amassed a considerable amount of money single-handedly by leveraging her uncanny investment abilities. Interestingly, Suzanne knew that she needed to factor both her hunches and the nation's emotional climate (Consumer Confidence Index) into her analysis of the stock market, but she didn't see how she needed to use all these skills in her love life. Irresistibly charming, with a French accent, she attracted attention easily, but soon intimidated the men she met because of her accomplishments and independence. Divorced for fifteen years, she was in and out of a quasi friendship/relationship with a kind but unambitious man. Occasionally driven by LUST BLINDNESS, she impulsively took up with more complex and less kind men to find some excitement.

But Suzanne had a softer side. She loved animals and older people, and she really wanted a long-term partner in her life. We spent a great deal of time discussing what was possible if she could only believe it. Using the Meant2Be Process, I tried to help her understand the importance of being able to define the qualities of a man with whom she could be happy.

Suzanne moved away and we lost touch. Then about a year later we bumped into her at the post office near where we live. She was looking typically stunning and sleek in a fashionable leather pantsuit and she wasted no time waving her hand in front of us so we could see her engagement ring. She hugged and thanked me for helping her realize all she deserved, and for showing her how to define and imagine a life with a wonderful man, the man that she met a few months after she moved away. He was also successful in business, his kids were grown up, and he found Suzanne to be the achievement-oriented kind of person he had always been looking for. His lifestyle required a great deal of travel, something both of them really enjoyed. They met through friends, and she sensed he was the one after their second date. After going together for almost a year, they were to be married in a few months.

Have you ever imagined your life with a special person, just the way you would like it to be? If not, you are missing a wonderful way to build belief, boost morale, and maximize the power of your unconscious mind as it brings your EMOTIONAL-SNAPSHOT and special person to life.

Use the Power of Your Mind to Achieve Your Goals

When I was developing the Meant2Be Process to help me find a lasting love, I realized that as an emotionally sensitive person and intuitive thinker I needed to balance those skills with some sound, logical thinking. My husband, Robert, on the other hand, put primarily his analytic thinking into his mate-finding efforts. He now realizes that he needed to balance analysis with developing emotional sensing skills and intuitive thinking. From my experience in the corporate world, I knew I needed to combine analytical, emotional sensing skills, and intuitive skills to help me in my quest. The technique I developed, the Meant2Be Process, works on all these levels: the analytical (business) level, the emotional (sensing) level, and the unconscious (intuitive, or gut) level. Whether you are primarily a logical thinker, or someone who makes decisions based primarily on feelings, or someone who listens to your instincts, the Meant2Be Process will help you use your analytical, emotional, and unconscious thinking more effectively to bring the right person into your life.

To develop your Meant2Be Profile and EMOTIONAL-SNAPSHOT you relied on analysis and emotion. Your unconscious may have been at work, and you may have been aware of thoughts coming into your head that seemed to make sense at a deeper level. Now we're going to focus on the crucial role your unconscious thinking plays in bringing your right one into your life, for the unconscious mind is where the magic happens behind the scenes.

Your mind is like a radio, receiving a virtually limitless range of stations. You may not even know these signals exist, but they are out there. Most of the time, there is so much interference from the outside world, and our own thoughts, that we can't hear the signals coming in through our unconscious mind. The great thing is that the unconscious mind never shuts down; it's always working for you.

Think of the unconscious mind as a huge reservoir. We are aware of knowledge at the shallow levels of water. But there are much deeper levels of water that contain knowledge we are not aware of—creative flashes, solutions to problems, talents.

There is empirical, scientific evidence of the existence of the "mysterious guiding hand" we call intuition or instinct. The American Heritage College Dictionary, defines intuition as *The act or faculty of knowing or sensing without the use of rational processes; immediate cognition.* However, this definition is no longer considered totally accurate. Scientists have found that the mind needs preparation and information before the imaginative flash, insight, or intuitive thought can occur.

The work you do on your Meant2Be Profile prepares your unconscious mind to be the "guiding hand" that will help you bring the right person into your life.

The greatest minds, the Mozarts, Da Vincis, and Einsteins, all found their inspiration in listening to their unconscious mind. Mozart heard music in his head before he tried to compose. Da Vinci dreamed of his inventions before he considered them possible. Einstein found the missing pieces to complete his great theories while lost in the strains of melody from the violin he played. They all believed in their abilities, and they believed in the possibility of achieving their goals through letting their unconscious mind help them.

The intuitive mind will tell the thinking mind where to look next.

—Dr. Jonas Salk

How Business Leaders Use the Unconscious

In this day of analysis and measurement of business effectiveness, it may be difficult for you to see the value of seemingly abstract concepts such as using the unconscious mind. Read what Stephen Covey and other business gurus have to say on the importance of having a vision and listening to your instincts.

> *The conflict between intuition and linear, nonsystematic thinking has planted the seed that rationality itself is opposed to intuition. This view is demonstrably false if we consider the synergy of reason and intuition that characterizes virtually all great thinkers.*
>
> *—Peter M. Senge, The Fifth Discipline*

Many companies don't realize the importance of time and space to access the unconscious and trigger the imagination. I frequently encountered this paradox in my consulting work. Often, the number one priority of an organization was for everyone to be capable of making decisions more effectively. The companies wanted to eliminate "analysis paralysis." But they translated effectiveness to simply mean making decisions faster and didn't focus on the quality of the decisions. The companies assumed the creative problem solving inherent in effective decision making was not an effective use of time.

A company may have all the numbers laid out and still be unsure of the cause of a problem. Experienced managers in touch with their intuition may sense that certain performance indicators are masking deeper problems, that something is going on beyond what the numbers show. These hunches can help locate the root causes of problems.

Studies of business leaders indicate that the key attributes that contribute to their success include the ability to balance analytical and intuitive thinking. Bob Lutz, former president of Chrysler, turned his struggling company around to become *Forbes Magazine's* 1996 Company of the Year. *Forbes* called the Chrysler team "Smart, Disciplined and Intuitive." Lutz says he was on a personal crusade to legitimize right brain, intuitive thinking in his company.

> Companies who are on the leading edge know that they need to allow their people the time and opportunity to activate unconscious thinking. They have learned that this form of intelligence, when factored in with analysis, makes for wiser decisions. This results in strategies that put them ahead of their competition—and they still have ample time to get their new products to market.

Imaging Possibilities

How does unconscious thinking apply to your search for that special person? When I was developing the Meant2Be Process and felt lonely or discouraged, I found it immensely satisfying to think about how it would feel to be with my special person, the person I had given life to through my Meant2Be Profile and EMOTIONAL-SNAPSHOT. I wrote about the things he and I would share, the places we would go, and how we would laugh together. Eventually I started to see little scenes in my mind. These thoughts and images made me feel less lonely and less discouraged. I started to really believe and then to know that I could have this person in my life, and I acted like I already knew him.

> It was no coincidence that the man I described in my journal—six months before I met him—turned out to be the man I married. My unconscious mind knew he existed long before my rational mind thought it possible.

But what if your imaging skills feel a bit rusty? For some of us, using our imagination seems as natural as putting one foot in front of the other to propel ourselves forward. But if your education and work reward you mainly for using your analytical skills, the parts of your mind that produce pictures and trigger your imagination may be a bit out of shape. And, as the saying goes, if you don't use it, you will lose it. Luckily, mental muscles can be conditioned back into shape. It just takes a little practice, and soon you'll see your innate skills return.

When you were a child, you may have made up games in your head and acted them out. Maybe you had imaginary friends, or you drew the pictures you could see in your mind. Then in school you were taught to pay attention, and that required you to use your conscious mind to focus. Unfortunately, you may have been taught that when you were not in this conscious state you were not thinking or learning.

How does this play out in the real world? At work you use your conscious mind to listen to a problem so that you can focus on everything someone or something is communicating to you. Then subconsciously you weigh all sides of the problem. If you are uncomfortable with uncertainty, feel pressured by time, or don't trust your instincts, you may stop at the subconscious level and force yourself to find a quick solution. But, if you give yourself time to reflect, you will access the richest part of your thinking: your unconscious mind. This is where you come up with that great "out-of-the-box" solution that really solves the problem—the same type of solutions that occur in leading-edge companies.

In reality, when you "daydream" (tune into your unconscious) your brain takes time to process information, store it, and dream up new possibilities. In this unconscious thinking state you can look at a problem upside down or any way you choose. You can see many possibilities and answers from a perspective that you would have never been able to access with your feet placed squarely on the ground in your conscious, logical thinking, analytical mode.

It's in this unconscious state of mind that artists, inventors, scientists, and effective business people show their remarkable curiosity and creativity. And it's in this state of mind that you can access all the wonderful thoughts and images associated with having your special person in your life. Accessing information this way will fuel all your efforts with "vitamin-fortified" mind power and will make you a more effective problem solver and decision maker at work and in every area of your life.

Access Your Unconscious Mind

Experts, like Dawna Markova, Ph.D., in her book, *No Enemies Within,* claim that everyone connects to their unconscious mind and imagination using primarily their visual (sight), auditory (hearing) or kinesthetic (touch and motion) senses.

> To effectively imagine what it feels like to have your special person in your life you need to determine which senses—seeing, hearing, or touching—will help you access your unconscious mind most easily.

If music is your muse, then listening to certain types of music will help you switch off your logical mind and shift gears to cruising speed. Maybe you need to be dancing to this music to fully shut off your analytical mind. You may enjoy gardening or woodworking and find that you can lose all sense of time and space as you become fully occupied by using your hands. If looking at the ocean or clouds in the sky brings you peace and relaxation, maybe this is the way you access your unconscious thinking, letting yourself fully experience what your eyes are seeing. You might do this sitting down or walking or running, while your eyes take in the visual stimulation.

Years ago I had the most incredible experience. While I was running, *Madame Butterfly* came on my radio headphones at the same time that I saw a rainbow fill the sky. Talk about a shift in consciousness—I didn't feel my feet touch the ground during that experience! My husband Robert says that when he is sailing, he scans the horizon and uses his body to sense the motion of the boat caused by the wind and the waves. This takes him away to a place where he can shut off his naturally analytical mind and just feel, imagine, and come up with ideas. He reports a similar experience when he is riding his motorcycle away from traffic.

You probably already know which of your senses will help you switch off your conscious thinking, what helps you relax and shift your mind and body into another dimension. If not, have some fun and experiment using different ways to trigger your senses.

(You'll find some ideas under "Access Your Intuitive Images" on the next page.) Notice how and when your mind starts to wander, time slows down, and you feel calmer. Identify which of your senses you like to use the most, but understand also that people with different sensory triggers receive and understand imagery differently.

For example, as a visual—auditory person, when I'm searching for answers I notice song lyrics. Phrases and stories pop into my mind. I write them down so I can see them, and that helps me understand them. Robert, however, is primarily kinesthetic. When he's searching for answers, he prefers asking questions, and then when he's active—walking, or doing some other physical activity—the answers flash across his unconscious.

Next time you are going to use your special way to escape (visually, or through sound, or touch and motion), ask yourself this question: How do I want to feel when I am with this special person that I'm bringing into my life? Now, put yourself into that wonderful, sensory environment and just enjoy the experience, without any further questioning.

Access Your Intuitive Images

If you are primarily:

Visual
Go to art galleries, look at pictures in magazines, meditate on nature, sit and watch people, watch music videos (with or without the sound)

Auditory
Listen to music, inspirational tapes, books on tape, the sound of the wind in the trees

Kinesthetic
Draw, paint, walk, run, dance, sail, bike, garden, sculpt, carve, build Legos, stroke your pet, strum a guitar or cello

Dual Sensory
Combine the appropriate activities

Later, when you come back to earth, you'll use your special way (described on the next page) to receive and understand your unconscious thoughts and images. You'll know how you want to feel with your right one. The clarity of your EMOTIONAL-SNAPSHOT will emerge and deepen every time you submerge into your subconscious.

77

Understand and Find Answers in Your Intuitive Images

If you are primarily:

Visual   Write or draw whatever comes to mind

Auditory   Find someone to talk to about your images

Kinesthetic   Engage in a physical activity while you search for answers

Dual Sensory   Combine the appropriate activities

Practice Using Your EMOTIONAL-SNAPSHOT

You now have your EMOTIONAL-SNAPSHOT *firmly embedded in your conscious and unconscious.* What's next? You need to learn how to use your EMOTIONAL-SNAPSHOT in real life. Don't be concerned—it just takes practice. Using your EMOTIONAL-SNAPSHOT is like learning a new language. You need to practice with people to become fluent. You can safely practice comparing the feelings in your EMOTIONAL-SNAPSHOT to the feelings you have with friends, family, and coworkers, people you already like and who like you. But don't let them know what you are doing—you don't want to make your practice people uncomfortable.

You are going to become skilled at recognizing and pinpointing the positive feelings that different people evoke in you.

Tuck your EMOTIONAL-SNAPSHOT in your "pocket" and let's start by playing a game in your mind. When you're around your practice people, notice how you feel. Compare these feelings to the EMOTIONAL-SNAPSHOT of images and feelings from your Meant2Be Profile. What is it about these practice people that makes you feel this way? Do they have characteristics similar to ones you identified in your Profile? With practice you will begin to identify some similarities that will clarify the kind of person you want in your life.

As you sharpen your sensing skills and get in touch with how you want to feel when you're with someone, you'll feel more confident. You'll start to value yourself more, and you'll be ready to use these techniques on real dates.

On page 109 you'll find an example from the Meant2Be DateBook. The DateBook will help you pinpoint how you feel with both practice people and real dates. If you are prone to falling in lust or over-romanticizing, seeing on paper how you feel about someone will help clarify your thinking and keep you on the straight and narrow. You'll learn more information about using the Meant2Be DateBook in Step 3. Go ahead and practice matching the feelings in your EMOTIONAL-SNAPSHOT to those you get when you are with your practice people.

7 Ways to Unleash Your Unconscious

Now that you've learned how to access your unconscious, intuitive thinking by using your visual, auditory, or kinesthetic senses, let's look at what you need to do to really make the power of your unconscious mind work for you as you go through the Meant2Be Process. People who are in touch with their unconscious mind describe a sequence of events that brings them in touch with their special person—a sequence of events that goes beyond coincidence.

Imagine

The technique of visualization means your senses create powerful mental images. Imagine what it feels like to have a person in your life who epitomizes the feelings generated by your Meant2Be Profile. Don't try to see the details of that face, but sense how you feel when that person is smiling at you. Imagine how it feels to hold them and be held in their arms, the twinkle in those loving eyes when they gently tease you. These images, the images and feelings that your Profile evokes, are your EMOTIONAL-SNAPSHOT that you keep in your "pocket" to remind you of how you want to feel when you are meeting with people. The more you can use your imagination to visualize, draw, or write about this person, the more your mind will start to believe.

One way to enhance the message your unconscious mind receives from visualization is to use music. Select a piece of your favorite music that evokes wonderful feelings and images when you listen to it. Each time you want to imagine how it feels to have that special person in your life (the one in your EMOTIONAL-SNAPSHOT) listen to that music. This music will become your "signature tune" for success. The inherent positive feelings from the music will jump-start your efforts, infusing your mind with stronger images.

See It in Your Mind—Achieve It in Your Life

In his book, *The Seven Habits of Highly Effective People,* Stephen R. Covey says that almost all world-class athletes and peak performers, such as astronauts, are visualizers.

Believe—Shut Off Your Critical Thinking

If you are a logical thinker, this is where you have to be willing to suspend your analysis. Did you know it is possible to think too much? In one of many scientific experiments that demonstrate this, a panel of experts was asked to rate a variety of wines. Then two groups of lay people were asked to rate the wines. Group A was told to just enjoy the wines and rate them later based on their gut reaction. Group B was told to use their best analytical skills to rate the wines. Group A rated the wines exactly as did the experts, while Group B rated none correctly.

This doesn't mean that analytical thinking is ineffective or wrong. It's the over-analyzing that shuts down the unconscious mind. In life we need to use all our thinking skills, analytical, emotional, and unconscious. But to imagine and sense your right one, you need to shut off your rational thinking. When you let your unconscious take over, this will happen.

Get Passionate

We know the unconscious mind is activated when you are dealing with your heart's desire and when you are passionate about your goals. When in your life have you felt really excited about the prospect of accomplishing something? Maybe it was taking a dream vacation or owning a new car or house, seeing your child achieve their dreams, or getting a plum promotion. As you thought about these things happening, as you read about and planned for them in your mind, did you notice that your excitement rose? Feel that same excitement, that passion, for the arrival of your special someone.

Feel the Music and the Passion

John, one of our students, dreams about having a partner in his life who can share his passion for dancing. He says that when he listens to the Strauss Waltzes he finds himself weaving wonderful pictures in his mind of waltzing with his special woman held firmly in his arms.

Let Go

One of the most important parts of this process is that you must let go of all the push, drive, and determination normally associated with reaching a goal. Have you ever tried to remember a word or a name and the more you thought about it, the more stuck you got? Then when you decide to forget about it, it pops into your mind. The unconscious mind has its own speed and schedule—you can not rush it. Forcing your attention on it doesn't work. So get in touch with all the wonderful feelings associated with meeting this special person, enjoy the feelings, but don't view the process as an exercise routine that you have to follow every day. Give your unconscious mind room to work.

Relax and Enjoy the Results

> One of our students said that when she was first
> working on this Process, she read the description
> in her EMOTIONAL-SNAPSHOT and repeated it
> several times a day like a mantra so that she could
> believe that her special man did exist. Finally she
> stopped pushing the Process this way and just
> enjoyed the feelings. Shortly after this change in
> attitude, she reported meeting a wonderful man.

So don't obsess about your EMOTIONAL-SNAPSHOT.
Wanting something so much or being so determined
can block your unconscious mind from working for
you. Give your unconscious mind room to work.

Hold onto the Feelings—
Let Go of the Expectations

Let your imagination go wild and enjoy the fantasies
and the feelings. But let go of the expectations about
timing—when this person has to appear. Let go of
expectations that the person you just met, or are going
to meet, has to be *the one*. I was guilty of doing this
with every man I met who seemed to fill some part of
my life that had been empty for so long. If you are
starved for affection and meet an affectionate person,
this alone is not a reason to believe that this is *the one*.
By staying tuned into your EMOTIONAL-SNAPSHOT you'll
unleash your unconscious so it can guide you to the
right one.

Be Open and Accept

If for some reason you're still dubious about using your unconscious mind as part of the Meant2Be Process, then keep a healthy dose of skepticism—and try it anyway. What have you got to lose? Nobody is going to know what you're doing. You may be pleasantly surprised by the results.

> The mind does not distinguish between reality and imagination. It absorbs all the stimuli it receives and responds with real emotions.

Take Action

You've got to take action. You have to be willing to try new things, follow hunches, and make the extra effort. It's like the old joke about the poor, devout woman who prayed to God, asking to win the lottery. She prayed every day, day and night, and still nothing happened. Eventually, God, seeing her faith and distress, spoke to her and said, "Agnes, do me a favor, please. At least meet me halfway—buy a lottery ticket." So take the necessary action. Attend a party or social activity, even though you may not be in the mood. Whether you think it is God's hand that will guide you, your intuition, or both, nothing is going to happen if you just sit around in your home or office, and wait.

To Activate Your Unconscious

- ■ Visualize

- ■ Believe this Person Exists

- ■ Get Passionate

- ■ Let Go

- ■ Hold onto the Feelings

- ■ Be Open

- ■ Take Action

You've tucked your Meant2Be Profile away for safe-keeping. You've created *your* EMOTIONAL-SNAPSHOT of the right person for you. You've practiced with family, friends, and coworkers to compare how you feel with people you like to feelings evoked by your EMOTIONAL-SNAPSHOT. You've let your unconscious guide you to all the wonders of being with your right one. You're ready to bring that special person into your life!

Step 3: Make Smart Choices to Attract the Right People

Who Has Time to Find the Right Person?

Everybody, no matter how gorgeous they look or how successful they are, at some time or other has trouble meeting compatible people. Movie stars and corporate moguls feel vulnerable just like the rest of us mere mortals when it comes to meeting new people.

It isn't just who you meet—where you meet affects how you feel with a person. I used to have to push myself out the door to meet men in settings that were not comfortable. The results were often disastrous for my self-esteem. I preferred meeting men for the first time in daylight. It wasn't a matter of safety so much as that I am happier doing things in the daylight. Trust me, it doesn't hurt to see what someone looks like in natural light either.

> It's important to find ways to meet people that minimize our innate anxiety and allow us to appear at our relaxed best.

I have also come to understand that some of the anxiety in meeting new people comes from our need to feel desired—what if I put myself out there and no one wants me? Sometimes we are so anxious to find that special person, yet we wonder if they really exist. The antidote to this doubtful thinking is to recognize that it is just anxiety—it is not reality.

It Only Takes One

You do not need or even want everyone to want you. All you need is the right one at the right time.

One bozo arranged to meet me for the first time in front of a closed movie theatre so we could easily find each other. I stood there and waited. A car approached, with him obviously in it, slowed down in front of me, and drove on by. I've heard of drive-in dates, never drive-by ones. It helps to keep reminding yourself all you need is one right one while you are meeting and dating those wrong people.

It's natural for your confidence to get shaken when you're dating. Forget the "what ifs." Focus on the reality: You now know what makes you happy. You know this kind of person does exist. You are going to find each other.

Get a Good Return on Your Financial and Emotional Investments

If you have been out of the dating scene for some time you may be wondering how evaluating ways to meet people is going to help you when you don't even know where to start. You didn't put your EMOTIONAL-SNAPSHOT in the drawer with your Meant2Be Profile, did you? Remember Step 2? Use your EMOTIONAL-SNAPSHOT to help you crystallize the feelings you get when you think about your special person. Then spend as much time as you can using your imagination to bring that special person to life in your mind and heart. The more you allow yourself to feel confident and elated at the prospect of meeting your special person, whom you know already exists, the more ready you will be to try new and different ways to meet this person.

Remember, you don't have to meet anyone until you are ready. Practice visualizing being with your right one and evaluate each dating resource. So when you are ready to begin meeting people who fit your criteria, you will already have decided which methods for meeting people make you feel the most comfortable. At first you may want to try more familiar environments, to gain confidence before trying something completely new or more costly.

Whether you are actively dating or have been out of the dating scene for some time, remember that you are now trying to meet as many *qualified* people as possible.

Tune into your unconscious, listen to your instincts, and:

■ Enjoy the company.

■ Keep in mind that most of the people you meet
and date will not be the right one.

■ Remember to practice saying no to the wrong
ones to make room for the right one.

Be Prepared for Opportunity

When you are clear on your goal and act like
you have already achieved it, life has a funny way
of creating the right timing and opportunities to
make it happen. All you have to do is be prepared.
That is what the Meant2Be Process does for you.

As if the emotional side of meeting people isn't already
difficult enough, the expenses incurred can make things
even more challenging. I spent thousands of dollars on
video dating clubs, matchmaking services, and special-
interest athletic clubs. It didn't even occur to me to
consider how well these dating resources would work
for me. I was blinded by a simple misconception.

Fact Not Fiction

Myth: If I could only meet enough people, then
eventually the right one will come along.

Reality: If you don't know what you are really
looking for in the first place, you will meet
lots of people who are not right for you.

91

Evaluate Dating Resources

In Step 1 of the Meant2Be Process, you defined the kind of person you want to bring into your life based on how you want to feel with that person (your Meant2Be Profile). Then in Step 2 you focused on how it feels to have this person in your life (your EMOTIONAL-SNAPSHOT). Now that you believe this kind of person exists, what is going to happen next?

Well, Ed McMahon is not going to ring your doorbell and say "Your dream person is here." You need to take action. You need to build awareness, so the right people know you exist. If you were putting a new product on the market, wouldn't you make sure that your message reached the right audience—that the time, money, and effort you expended would produce sales? You personally have even more at stake than a mere financial bottom line. But this time, using the Meant2Be Process, any risk will be worth it, because you are going to find someone with whom you can be truly happy.

> If you were looking to buy your ideal computer system, wouldn't you compare different options, prices, return polices, and after-purchase support? You need to use the same analysis and discernment when you are deciding which dating services to use.

Start by examining how you are currently meeting people. Are the people you are meeting this way the right kind of people for you? Even if they are, you may still want to try some other ways to meet people. You can decide which dating methods will work best for you by analyzing your choices, based on your personality, what makes you comfortable, and what you can afford. The Dating Resource Evaluator on page 94 is designed to help you decide which dating resources will give you the best financial and emotional return on your investment. If this seems too cold and calculating for you, keep in mind that if you are buying a car it is considered smart to read *Consumer Reports* and gather other information to get the best car at the best price, before you take your checkbook to the car dealer's lot.

Why should spending money on your love life be any less important? In Step 2 we focused on using the unconscious mind. Now you are going to put your analytical thinking to work where it will do the most good.

The Meant2Be Dating Resource Evaluator will help you decide where you want to be spending your time, emotional energy, and money to meet the right people. Create more columns if there are additional criteria that are important to you. Identify all the different types of dating services that you might consider. Then learn all that you can about each one using the six evaluation criteria discussed in the next section (and any others you may have added.)

Meant2Be - Dating Resource Evaluator						
	Cost	Demographics & Competition	Preview & References	Comfort & Convenience	Time Invested	Duration
Romance Print Ads						
Online Matchmaking						
Video Dating Clubs						
Matchmaking Services						
Activity & Special Interest Clubs						
Lunch & Dining Clubs						

Evaluation criteria are listed across the top and common dating resources are listed down the left side of the chart. The bottom rows are for other types of dating resources that you may want to explore.

Using the Dating Resource Evaluator

Before signing up with any dating service, carefully analyze all the following criteria and any others you want to consider. Record the information on your Dating Resource Evaluator so you will have all the facts in front of you as you decide which types of dating services and specific providers are best for you.

Cost

The actual cost of using any dating resource often goes well beyond the initial signup cost. Be sure to consider all associated costs, which may include items such as getting photos made, professional services such as makeup and hairstyling, individual event fees, special service fees, special clothing or equipment purchases, and renewal fees (when your initial membership term runs out). If there are other similar dating services available, compare the differences in total cost.

Demographics and Competition

This is where you put on your marketing hat to examine the kind of people the dating resource targets, who its membership consists of, and where you fit into its target market. Ask yourself, How many people will I have to compete with? Will this dating service allow me to meet people who fit my general criteria?

To meet the kind of person you've defined in your Meant2Be Profile, you need to start with fairly broad criteria and then get more selective. This is like having a fishing net with small holes that you cast out to sea. You initially capture a wide variety of fish. Then you select the ones you want. The net represents only your basic criteria, such as a broad age range, religion, ethnicity, and general types of people (athletic, artistic, intellectual, cultured)—not specific criteria. The less specific you are, the more fish you will have to choose from. But you need to make sure that the type of people you want to meet make up a reasonable number of the participants in any dating resource you consider.

With all dating services, you need to determine what types of people make up the current membership. This includes not only the type of people whom you are looking for, but also your potential competition in the membership—those who are similar to you in age, gender, economic profile, etc.

Are you a 38-year-old woman looking for a 36- to 46-year-old man and the club's membership primarily consists of 28- to 38-year-old guys? Are you a 43-year-old man looking for a 35- to 45-year-old woman and there are five men in their forties for every woman in your age range? In either case, you may have a very hard time getting the dates you want.

It is also important that you learn where the dating service is investing their advertising and marketing resources, so you will understand what types of new people it is attracting.

> Be smart and don't waste your time and resources looking for tuna where only the salmon are running.

Preview and References

You need to verify each dating service's claims and find out about its membership. Ask for references that you can call—*then call them*. But be aware that some dating services have "professional" references—friends and associates they use for this purpose. Your best source of references is the special events held by the dating service. Ask to attend one of these events. And when you do, observe who attends—what kind of people are active participants. Talk to members about their personal experiences with this dating resource.

Comfort and Convenience

Ask yourself these questions: How do I feel about meeting people this way? Are there any safety factors to be considered? Is it convenient for me to use this dating resource? Is it geographically desirable? Will the person who runs this service be easy to reach directly by phone if I have a question or problem?

Time Invested

How much time do you have to spend in order to meet enough of the right kind of people? If you use online dating, you may have more people to choose from, but you will have to spend a great deal of time screening to find the kind of people you want to meet. A good matchmaker on the other hand will do the initial screening for you.

Duration

Realistically, how long do you think it might take to meet enough qualified people so you can select the right one? This will depend on the number of people available and what type of access you have to them. Video dating, for example, may provide more people, with easier access, than an introduction service.

Select the Best Dating Service Providers

In the Consumer Advice Section, which starts on page 133, you will find information on how to select and best use each of the types of dating services listed on your Dating Resource Evaluator:

- Romance Print Ads

- Online Matchmaking

- Video Dating Clubs

- Matchmakers/Introduction Services

- Activity and Special-Interest Clubs

- Lunch and Dining Clubs

This Consumer Advice information will help you determine which types of dating services will work best for you, based on the six criteria discussed in the previous section. Then it will help you investigate and select the best providers of each type of dating services you select. Remember to record all information on your Dating Resource Evaluator as you go through your provider selection process. Don't just rely on your feelings or intuitive thinking. In Step 3 of the Meant2Be Process, you need to employ all your logical, analytical thinking skills.

Where and How Do You Meet People?

There are unlimited ways to meet people. Here we discuss a few of the most common approaches. Whether you choose a simple method to meet people, such as attending a singles' group affiliated with your house of worship, or something more daring, like a singles' cruise, the Meant2Be evaluation process can be applied to any method used to meet people.

Remember, you need to maximize the effectiveness of each way you choose to meet people so that you are meeting more of the qualified people whom you will want to get to know better. Once you select the best dating services for you, you'll use your EMOTIONAL-SNAPSHOT as a way to recognize the right people for you. (This is covered in detail on page 55.)

Your EMOTIONAL-SNAPSHOT will help you recognize the right one among all the other people who may jumpstart your heart and hormones. By using several different methods concurrently to meet people you can broaden your possibilities. Only you can decide how much time and money to dedicate to meeting people and getting to know them.

General Guidelines for Using Any Dating Resource

■ As you meet people, remember to stay in touch with the *3-C's—Compatibility, Connection,* and *Comfort—* and use a date book (see page 109) to keep track of how you feel with the people you are dating.

■ No one dating resource can do it all. To meet the greatest number of qualified people, use more than one method.

■ Do not alter your normal style of dress, meeting place, or preferred meeting time if it makes you feel less than comfortable.

■ Just because someone is interested in you, it does not mean you have to meet this person. When your instincts say no, listen to them and act accordingly.

■ Research, research, research before signing any contract or committing any money.

■ Get standard rates and cancellation policies in writing. Take them home to read before signing anything.

■ Are salespeople commissioned? If so, negotiate in order to avoid paying a premium price. "This day only" specials are often not the least expensive deal.

■ Do not be blinded by pictures of attractive people or stories of successful clients.

■ Attend events as a guest and talk to members before signing any contract.

■ Also consider the value of making new friends through an activity or dining club—friends can provide a network to introduce you to other singles.

■ Talk to dating service competitors. Compare prices and services—you may indeed get what you pay for. Less expensive is not always a better choice.

■ Any dating service is there to provide you with access to qualified people who meet your criteria— not to help you sustain a relationship.

Meet a "Better Quality" of People

Let's start with the assumption that you have defined the kind of people you want to meet by identifying the broadest criteria possible. If you remember, earlier we compared broad criteria to a fishing net. The broader the criteria—the smaller the holes—the more fish you capture in the net.

You don't want all these fish. You don't have the time or the inclination to try all of them—some wouldn't be to your taste. So you will have to decide which are the best fish for you and throw the others back into the sea.

Now you need your EMOTIONAL-SNAPSHOT to help you sift through your net full of possibilities.

Remember, you are not going to use the details from your Meant2Be Profile as a template to measure everyone. You are going to use your EMOTIONAL-SNAPSHOT—the feelings that your Profile generates in you when you imagine having this special person in your life—to determine which of the people you date might be right for you.

Say you imagined an independent, adventuresome, affectionate person, with a great sense of humor. You saw yourself with them backpacking in exotic places, laughing in the Louvre, snuggling in a sleeping bag, flying in a plane that they pilot. Now, it is important to

103

remember that you are not necessarily looking for someone who mentions flying planes or sleeping under the stars. You are looking for someone who probably would like to try these things. Your goal is to find someone with the energy and style that fits these feelings. Determining if someone is right for you is not an analytical process; it is intuitive, a gut instinct—you will know it when you feel it. You will trust your instincts because you've practiced with your EMOTIONAL-SNAPSHOT. *You already know how it feels to be with your right one.*

Take your EMOTIONAL-SNAPSHOT, the images and feelings you generated in your Meant2Be Profile, with you as you meet people through everyday activities, through business and social functions, and through friends and others. Take these images and feelings with you as you scan the Internet or read romance print ads, review videos or member profiles. Take along your EMOTIONAL-SNAPSHOT as you meet people at activity or dining clubs. Take the images and feelings generated by your Meant2Be Profile and use them to create an ad for the Internet or newspaper, or when you are writing your profile for a dating club. Take the images and feelings with you when you are working with matchmakers so they can understand the kind of person you want to meet.

Now that you've spread your net and attracted people with more potential, it's time to learn how to recognize the ones who have the most potential. In the next section you will discover how to use a special tool we have designed to help you achieve this very important purpose.

Go from Dating to Relating

A common question we hear from our students at Meant2Be Seminars is "How long should I date someone to find out if this is going anywhere and does the three-date minimum work?" I do not believe in rigid rules, like giving someone at least three dates. At a minimum, you want to spend time with people you enjoy. You're not looking for rockets or violins at first, but you at least want to have a pleasant time. If you feel irritated, impatient, or just plain ready to bolt, why would you want to see this person two more times! That said, first dates can be uncomfortable for anyone. You need a way to pinpoint how you feel *about yourself* when you are on your dates and to understand how that changes over time as you get to know the other person.

That's how a date book can help you. (On page 109 you will see a sample page from the Meant2Be DateBook). Whenever you have positive feelings from a date, record the name of the person you dated in your date book, what you did together, and how you felt with this person. Rate your date using the *3-C's* (*Compatibility, Connection, and Comfort*) plus *Chemistry*, because after all you can not deny the role physical attraction has in your dating choices. If you are a person who has a tendency toward LUST BLINDNESS your datebook will help you see things more clearly.

Next, compare your EMOTIONAL-SNAPSHOT to the feelings

you had on your date. How close does your date seem to your EMOTIONAL-SNAPSHOT? Also write about any other impressions you have about that date.

Keep in mind you are only recording dates with people where there have been some positive feelings—people you want to go out with again. Do not reinforce the negative—let those experiences go. Over time, as you continue to date someone, you'll notice changes in your ratings. This will help you decide where the relationship is going, where you want it to go, and whether you want to continue it.

EMOTIONAL-SNAPSHOT + DateBook = Better Relationship Potential

Dave is dating Kathy. Over the last six weeks they have gone out eight times. On his first dates with Kathy, Dave rated *Compatibility* and *Comfort* as needing more time to know how he felt. *Connection* and *Chemistry* were on target. He indicated that with an exclamation point. He and Kathy were definitely attracted to each other. They both came from the Midwest and were career focused, so there was *Connection*, but it was too soon to tell if they were *Compatible*. *Comfort* wasn't there yet because Dave thought that they were too on edge from all the physical chemistry. Then Dave compared the feelings he had with Kathy to his EMOTIONAL-SNAPSHOT. In his Meant2Be Profile he had written about wanting to be with a woman with whom he could feel relaxed, someone who would soothe him and help him calm down from his hectic business life. Dave had a history of being involved with women with whom he had a lot of immediate attraction. Those relationships tended to burn out fairly quickly.

Dave met Terri through a friend at Toastmasters. After a great phone conversation with Terri, he was excited at the prospect of meeting her because she had such a husky, sexy voice. The intensity of the physical chemistry they had on the phone wasn't quite there when they first met, but Dave loved Terri's blue eyes and her great smile when she laughed. In fact he couldn't remember having so much fun with someone in a long time. While he rated their beginning *Chemistry* as low, the *Comfort* and *Connection* he had with Terri were strong. After another date or two with her, he realized that his feelings about Terri initially had been too focused on the intensity of his physical response to her, and that now he did in fact find her quite attractive.

Dave had been doubtful that he could find the woman in his EMOTIONAL-SNAPSHOT and also be attracted to her. By dating both Kathy and Terri, and tracking his responses to both of them, he was able to distinguish between his old patterns of falling in lust and his emerging awareness of what he really wanted.

Dave decided to give more time to getting to know Kathy and Terri to see how things changed over time. For the first time in his dating history since his divorce, he was aware of not only how he felt with the woman he was dating, but also how he wanted to feel.

Sample Page from the Meant2Be DateBook:

Meant2Be DateBook

Name	Date No.	Comfort Feeling Rating (1–10)	Connection Feeling Rating (1–10)	Compatibility Feeling Rating (1–10)	Chemistry Feeling Rating (1–10)	Emotional-Snapshot Feeling Rating (1–10)
Kathy Thomas	1	Comments: Kathy's from the Midwest too—liked her traditional values. Definitely lit my fire! Couldn't sleep when I got home—too keyed up.				
Terri Siegal	1	Comments: Sounds great on the phone—but didn't look quite like I imagined. But I loved her sense of humor. A little chemistry. Quite relaxed.				
Kathy	2	Comments: Still sizzling but I'm not too sure about our long-term goals—she really seems to want to move back to Midwest and I sure don't. Comfort is still not there.				
Terri	2	Comments: Felt so relaxed with Terri—the more I get to know her the more I like being with her. We seem to have a lot in common—nice to feel I can just be myself.				

Step 4: Deal with Your Heart and Hormones

Why Can't I Be Attracted to the Right People?

Why Do They Call Them Love Songs?

To unrequited love and burning desire,
To please, baby, light my fire,
To John and Paul, Tina and Ray,
To Mick and Barbra, and Jose,
I cried when I heard your song
How can love be so right,
when I feel this wrong?

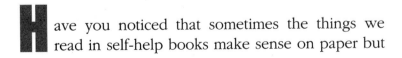 ave you noticed that sometimes the things we read in self-help books make sense on paper but

are difficult to apply to real life? Techniques for meeting and recognizing the right kind of person will be useful only if they work when you are deeply affected by your heart and hormones.

You can not deny, nor should you stop enjoying, the pleasures of attraction and romance. That is part of the complexity of chemistry we talked about in Step 1 of the Meant2Be Process. So, if you want to be lusty and romantic while having no illusions about *compatibility* and the real reason you are together, then go ahead and enjoy yourself. However, having serious intentions about a relationship that is no more than a romantic illusion or lustful adventure can get you into serious trouble.

Everyone, no matter what age or how many years they've been dating, needs practice at recognizing the right people and saying no to the wrong ones. Just like chocolate cake can test the will power of the best of us, certain people will tempt us with LUST BLINDNESS or ROMANTIC FANTASIA. I used to suffer from both these maladies. And I remember how I used to be jolted back into a painful reality when the other person made it clear that he did not want the depth of relationship I had imagined we both wanted. As another example, one of our students was feeling down about her job. She succumbed to LUST BLINDNESS with someone who had been explicitly straightforward about not wanting any type of relationship with her or anyone at that time. She knew she would be getting nothing back, other than a brief good time, but she didn't realize it would be quite as brief as it turned out. She felt lonelier than before she had met the man. It seems that whether you binge on men or women or cake to feel better about yourself, you can feel pretty lousy the next morning.

PREMATURE EXPECTATION is another way we can sabotage our chances of having a good relationship. PREMATURE EXPECTATION is different from positive anticipation because of the inherent over-the-top excitement and overwhelming anxiety that it produces.

Of course it is normal and human to experience LUST BLINDNESS, ROMANTIC FANTASIA, and PREMATURE EXPECTATION. And chances are you will be faced with all three of these challenges as you expand your dating possibilities in an effort to meet the right person. Awareness is your best protection. So here are the keys to diagnosing and curing these dating maladies. Treatment is not a matter of denial. It is simply a matter of staying focused on the *3-C's* and using your EMOTIONAL-SNAPSHOT to keep an eye on your ultimate goal: having a loving, lasting relationship with someone who likes you just the way you are.

PREMATURE EXPECTATION

It's been ages since you had someone special in your life. You met briefly at a party, were fixed up by friends or a matchmaker, or found someone through the personals, and you have talked on the phone to them for hours, late into the night. You have laughed and shared parts of yourself that you haven't shared in a very long time. You may even have called this person back, and had more long, intimate conversations. You feel excited and almost giddy with anticipation. You've decided *this is it.*

But by the time you finally go to meet this person, you are a combination of nervous excitement and stone-cold fear that this person may not like you when they see you or get to know you. If you haven't even seen a picture of the person yet, you've developed your own picture of what the person looks like, what you *want* the person to look like. Then you meet; and even if this person's looks don't disappoint you (or your looks don't disappoint them), the easy rapport and laughter you shared on the phone are nowhere to be found.

Now what?

> Don't spend a long time on the phone with anyone before you meet them in person.

You see, there is something very intimate and safe about talking on the phone, especially late at night when you are each lying in your bed with little if any clothes on sharing your innermost thoughts. This is fine when you already know someone. But you are talking to a stranger! The same can be said of e-mail relationships. You can develop very intimate connections with people without even knowing their true age or gender. Even if you have verified information, spending a great deal of time talking or writing and baring your soul to someone before you meet can result in PREMATURE EXPECTATION and serious disappointment.

If you are a highly visual person who lets your imagination run wild before you meet someone, then romance print ads or the Internet may not work very well for you. You may find singles' clubs or video dating, where you can see and hear someone, more effective. If you still build up your expectations, even after you have just met someone briefly, you may also be suffering from LUST BLINDNESS or ROMANTIC FANTASIA.

One way to safeguard yourself from PREMATURE EXPECTATION is to date different people for different reasons and varying interests while remaining clear on your and their intentions. When you are overly anxious, because you want someone to be "the one," you tend to attract people who may take advantage of your vulnerability. And when you are needy the right types of men or women tend to run the other way. This was a hard reality for me to learn, because I grew up believing that I should always be a one-man woman, and that there was something inherently unethical about dating more than one person at a time. In addition, I wanted to believe that I was the only person in someone's life. I later found that when I told the men I dated that I was at the discovery stage, seeing different people and finding out what I wanted in a long-term partner, this freed both of us to get know and enjoy each other without all the pressure. Of course, I wanted the other person to be at a discovery stage too. Nobody wants to date someone who has a passionate, ongoing connection with someone else. And, if you have a tendency to get physically involved with someone too soon, dating several people at the discovery stage will help you hold off on that aspect of a relationship until you are really ready to take that important step into another level of intimacy.

> When your life is full of enjoyable activities and good people to share them with, you are less likely to scare off the right person by being overly anxious or appearing needy.

Being overly anxious seems to keep company with PREMATURE EXPECTATION. It's OK to just date for fun and companionship while you seek your one true love. On the other hand, if you postpone dating until you think you've found that one true love, that someone you believe to be your ideal person, you may find yourself lonely and more prone to disappointment.

So, use the Meant2Be Process to help you improve the quality of people you bring into your life, whether they become just friends, shorter-term romantic interests, or the ultimate one.

Recognizing PREMATURE EXPECTATION:

■ You spend a lot of time fantasizing about what a person looks like before you meet them.

■ You experience anxiety waiting for them to call you back.

■ You feel irritated or overly disappointed when they don't seem to express the same amount of interest in meeting you that you have in meeting them.

■ You build people up to be more than they turn out to be-or could be.

The Antidote to PREMATURE EXPECTATION:

■ Date people for different reasons.

■ Don't spend a long time on the phone or writing e-mails before meeting each other.

■ Get to know a variety of people who embody different attributes and interests.

■ Forget scarcity thinking that says that you had better make this one the right one because there may be no more—think about choice, variety, fun.

■ Go back to Step 2 and reread the tips for letting go and letting things happen.

117

ROMANTIC FANTASIA

Imagine you and someone you adore are going down a river in a canoe. You are doing almost all the paddling. And although you are tired and often have to compensate for the lack of your date's paddling, you tell yourself that it's all right, you can keep the canoe on course by yourself. No matter how tired you get, or how much help you need to keep the canoe from going off course, your date lets you do all the work. And you're still telling yourself that it is all right. This is ROMANTIC FANTASIA.

The next time you are in a romance-based relationship ask yourself: Do I plan most, if not all, of our dates? Am I the one who sends most, if not all, of the cards? Am I the one who does the little thoughtful things needed to keep the relationship afloat? If so, you are probably suffering from ROMANTIC FANTASIA. Try putting the oars down and see if the other person will row for a change.

Online Intimacy—Off Line Reality

Barbara-Jean is a very attractive, full-size woman with an enthusiastic, action-oriented personality. Friendly, inquisitive, and outgoing she immediately likes just about everyone she first meets. It wasn't surprising then that she sailed through the Meant2Be Process with ease and developed an EMOTIONAL-SNAPSHOT that she internalized quickly.

She was ready to get out and meet Mr. Right as quickly as she could. Using the Internet she connected to people easily and met a man who was as interested in meeting her as she was in meeting him. Not long after they started going out, she told us enthusiastically about going on a hike with him and talking intimately about a future together. Things move fast for Barbara-Jean. Then, not long after, she found out that he was back online trying to meet someone else—she was devastated. She was blaming herself, wondering if it was her size or something she said that brought this about. She pursued him via e-mails for a while, not recognizing that he had pulled away. Whatever his reasons, they weren't important. She eventually understood that ROMANTIC FANTASIA, and its inherent desire for instant intimacy, was at fault. Unlike her previous experiences, Barbara-Jean was able to easily get herself back on track and refocused by recalling her EMOTIONAL-SNAPSHOT and the 3-C's. Instead of continuing to beat herself up for being the wrong size or the wrong personality, she was able to let go and continue on, with renewed hope.

My heart went out to Barbara-Jean as I recalled doing exactly the same thing with some man I met through the romance print ads. I overreacted too. I wrote him a letter blasting him with my outrage at his deception and apparent disloyalty. The poor guy, we had only been going out a few weeks. I wish I had developed the Meant2Be Process back then.

Recognizing ROMANTIC FANTASIA:

■ Fantasy takes over reality.

■ Your life revolves around waiting to hear from them and being with them.

■ When they don't call, you spin into depression.

■ You are the one sending the cards, writing the notes, and suggesting romantic dates—it's like being in a canoe and you are the only one paddling.

■ Everyone else can see that this person doesn't treat you well, but you always have plenty of rationalizations.

The Antidote to ROMANTIC FANTASIA:

■ Remember your EMOTIONAL-SNAPSHOT and the kind of person you know will contribute to your happiness—does this person really fit your snapshot?

■ Apply the *3-C's.*

■ You may believe that you have some cosmic *Connection,* but what about *Comfort*—can you really just be yourself, without trying to please the other person?

■ Would your time together survive reality tests, such as being sick, depressed, or bad-tempered?

■ What is the real basis for *Compatibility*—is your attraction based on just one thing, e.g., both of you wanting to live in Spain?

LUST BLINDNESS

LUST BLINDNESS probably needs little explanation. It's most likely to strike if you have been in a dating desert. You know you have LUST BLINDNESS when your whole dating life revolves around the proverbial bedroom where everything is wonderful. Your hormones are happy but the rest of you wants more: more time, more in common, more consideration. Everyone else in your life can see the lack of balance in the relationship, but *you* are in denial, or addiction.

There is an antidote for LUST BLINDNESS and ROMANTIC FANTASIA. Focus on the *3-C's*: *Compatibility, Connection,* and *Comfort*. Ask yourself, What is missing? The answers will definitely be *Compatibility,* and to some extent, *Comfort.* Then, as with PREMATURE EXPECTATION, go back and recall the EMOTIONAL-SNAPSHOT that your Meant2Be Profile generates. Repeat the visualization exercises so you get in touch with how it feels to have the right person in your life. Luxuriate in the feelings until you are confident again that you *can* have the right person in your life. Then you will be strong enough to let go of the relationships that are wrong for you.

121

Recognizing LUST BLINDNESS:

■ Sex is the driving force of the relationship yet you know you want more than just the physical.

■ You aren't being treated the way you want to be outside the bedroom, but you feel powerless to leave.

■ Honestly, how much do you know about this person—do you like who they really are?

The Antidote to LUST BLINDNESS:

■ Ask yourself, apart from excitement and raw attraction, how do I feel when I am with this person—anxious, unbalanced, bored, needy?

■ Compare these feelings to how you want to feel with the right person.

■ Think about the last time you had this kind of relationship and you finally saw the person for who they truly were, apart from the physical attraction. How did you feel then?

■ Apply the *3-C's*:

   ■ You know you have Chemistry—what about real *Compatibility, Comfort* and *Connection?*

   ■ Can you just be yourself with this person? Do they understand you, and do you understand them at a meaningful level?

Before I developed the Meant2Be Process, I felt that I had to hold on to the wrong people because I was not sure that there was anyone better out there who would want me. When I finally realized I deserved better, I found the strength to risk being alone again and let go of someone who was wrong for me. This is how I made room in my life to meet Robert.

If your heart were like an attic where you store attachments to old or wrong relationships, what would yours look like? Is it cluttered with outdated things? Clear it out, clean it up, polish it, open the windows, and let the light pour in. Then you will be ready for this special place to hold new treasures, not old regrets.

Happy Endings

When Is Mr. or Ms. Right Going to Appear?

You are probably asking yourself how long it will take to meet the right person using the Meant2Be Process. I met Robert six months after I started to use the techniques I am sharing with you. Remember, I was just developing the Process at that time, so it could happen even sooner for you. When I tell people in our classes that it took me six months to meet Robert, they laugh with recognition when I say most of us aren't sure we're going to meet the person in this lifetime, never mind in six months.

When You Are Ready

Remember my friend Suzanne? She had spent fifteen years since her divorce floundering in doubt and bad relationships. Once she got in touch with what she wanted, and knew it could happen, within months she connected with the man who became her life partner, someone who adored her just the way she was.

> *When the pupil is ready the teacher appears.*
>
> —*Zen saying*

When you have internalized how it feels to have the right person in your life, you will be ready to meet your right one.

When...

When you have prepared yourself by using the Meant2Be Profile to find out what makes you feel happiest in a relationship, when you have created and internalized your EMOTIONAL-SNAPSHOT, when you have put yourself out there in order to meet enough people, when you have practiced how to recognize how you feel with them, and when you have learned to say no to the wrong ones—then you will meet your right one.

In the meantime, you will meet a "better class" of people, people with whom you have much in common, people who like you just the way you are. There is another wise saying, "Where you plant your seeds, your garden will grow." Focus on the positive outcome of having the right person in your life. Fuel it with passion, and be clear about what you want. Let go of the need. You will have the lasting love of your life.

And, this time your relationship will withstand the normal ups-and-downs of life, bolstered by the strong foundation you have built on *Compatibility, Connection,* and *Comfort.*

126

When It Happens

When you have someone in your life who likes you just the way you are, and you feel the same about them, you'll find fewer reasons to fight over the silly stuff because you won't have basic incompatibilities that fuel these fights. You'll never have to worry (as I used to) that this person won't like you when they finally get to know you. Romantic feelings and attraction aside, the reason you are liked will stay secure, even when the person sees you at your worst. All the reasons that you find each other so wonderful will overshadow and minimize your less lovable parts.

I know all this for a fact. Despite my years of unsuccessful relationships, and Robert's failed marriages, we have seen how the *3-C's* work in our lives. Life has thrown us major curves this last few years—career demands, major medical problems, family issues—yet we continue to grow closer and remain each other's best friend.

Almost the End...But Really the Beginning

We want the same for you. You now know it is possible. You know that you deserve lasting love. It's time for you to use the Meant2Be Process to bring the right one into your life.

Dance with me naked in the night
Soft whispers in my hair
Me in your jacket
You in black tie
Melting honey kisses
Deep throated sigh

This concludes the first part of this book, which guided you through the 4-Step Meant2Be Process. In the next section, "Consumer Advice," you will find practical information and guidance that will help you meet and enjoy the company of people who have the qualities you identified in your Meant2Be Profile. The final section, "Dating Advice," addresses some of life's challenging dating situations, and gives you some practical advice for how to recognize and bring the right person into your life.

Your success is our greatest reward.

Please let me know how the Meant2Be Process

helped you find your special person.

Philippa Courtney
Meant2Be Unlimited
236 W. Portal Avenue, Suite 341
San Francisco, CA 94127

askphilippa@meant2be.com

Consumer Advice
Choose and Use Dating Resources Effectively

Consumer Advice

Choose and Use Dating Resources Effectively

A s we discussed in Step 3, you need to decide which dating service providers will work best for you by analyzing each resource, based on your style, what makes you comfortable, and what you can afford. As you go through this section remember to use the Dating Resource Evaluator on page 94.

This section contains information on six commonly used dating resources:

- Romance Print Ads

- Online Matchmaking

- Video Dating Clubs

- Matchmakers and Introduction Services

- Activity and Special-Interest Clubs

- Lunch and Dining Clubs

Romance Print Ads

1. Cost: Compared to using video dating, matchmakers, dining clubs, and other dating services, print romance ads are the least expensive method to attract and meet people. If you answer romance ads in the paper you only pay for each 900-service phone call. There is usually no charge to place a romance print ad unless you include extra lines or use bold headlines to make your ad stand out. But remember that cost is only one consideration in deciding which dating resource to try.

2. Demographics and Competition: Ask yourself who reads each newspaper that has romance ads. Most newspapers publish demographics of their readers; these include age ranges, work types and income information. But the easiest way to determine who reads the romance section is to scan the paper's personal ads and see how many of the advertisers fit the type of person you are targeting. And, how many of the ads are looking for the kind of people you are looking for? Also look at the general style of the publication; do you want upscale, conservative, creative, alternative, or wild? Does the paper's style fit yours?

3. Preview and References: This category does not apply to romance print ads.

4. Comfort and Convenience: Should you place an ad or respond to other people's ads? I've had lots of experience doing it both ways. As a woman, I liked placing an ad because it protected my identity. And in fact women tend to get more responses to romance ads than men do. Does that mean that men should not place ads? On the contrary, men should and do place romance ads, because they are more likely to get what they are looking for than if they simply responded to someone else's ad.

One of the realities of romance print ads is that people can not initially see what each other looks like. That can be good or bad, depending on your point of view. What is initially more important to you? Is it getting to know someone a little bit before seeing each other or is it seeing what each other looks like first?

I feel that romance ads are not the best place to look if you're someone who is preoccupied with packaging (both yours and theirs) or if you are seeking someone with a specific look. Why? Because people often overestimate how they look. Just about everybody says he or she is attractive; so if you're looking for a specific type or level of good looks, it is easy to be disappointed.

Years ago I remember seeing a romance ad for a man who described himself as being a McGyver look-alike, comparing himself to the leading role in a television series. Years later, long after the show was defunct, he was still describing himself that way. Unless you *are* someone's twin, don't say you look just like someone famous. This is rarely the best way to describe yourself. First, people may fail to see the resemblance. And, more often than not, the person you meet will be disappointed that you don't live up to the billing.

5. Time Invested: It can be reaffirming to call your mailbox and hear the voices of all the people who are interested in meeting you. On the other hand, placing the ad, screening the calls, and meeting many of these people can be a time-consuming and tiring process.

6. Duration: You may get to meet lots of people through the personals, but it can take quite a bit of time to screen all the possibilities and find the right person. You should also know that because there is only a small financial investment in placing an ad, people who are in transition from relationships or just looking to fill a temporary gap in their social lives often use the personals to get dates. If you are serious about finding one special person for a long-term relationship, you will need to carefully screen people so you don't waste time meeting the wrong ones. As part of your screening process, it's smart to find out how long it's been since this person has been in a relationship. Do you think it's important to know whether this person has recently come out of a significant relationship, whether they were the one leaving the relationship, or the one left behind? If asked by the person you are screening, how comfortable are you sharing the same kind of information about yourself?

Tips for Creating an Effective Romance Print Ad or Internet Profile

These tips can be used both for creating a print romance ad, discussed in the preceding section, and an Internet profile used in online matchmaking, a type of dating service that will be discussed in the next section. Don't forget that romance personals and Internet profiles are forms of advertising. Some people embellish themselves. If you're placing a personal ad, you should consider applying the common marketing principles that are used to develop effective product or business advertisements.

There are three key things you need to accomplish with a romance print ad or Internet profile:

- Get attention—that means getting the ad/profile read.

- Attract a broad enough range of responses. Remember the fishing net?

- Make sure your prospective right person can recognize him or herself in your ad or profile.

If you just talk about who you are and do a good job of making yourself sound attractive, you will get a big response, but you will also have to spend a lot of time screening all those people to find just the ones you really want to meet.

> Remember: You do not want a huge number
> of unqualified responses; you want just enough
> qualified people to choose from.

Save the more personal information and statements
about serious intentions for the voice mail message.
Find ways to differentiate yourself from the competition;
you can do this by being witty or by highlighting an
aspect of yourself that is interesting and different.

When Everyone Wants You but the Right One

Sylvia is an area manager for a clothing store chain.
As an army brat, she spent her childhood in various
countries overseas. Her exotic looks, refinement,
and intelligence make her highly desirable, yet she
prefers the anonymity of the Internet for finding a
prospective partner. She is concerned that if she
explains that she would like someone who is like
her, with exceptional looks and highly educated, she
would sound pretentious. While Sylvia finds the
enormous response to her profile affirming, she is
faced with screening all the men who are attracted
to her description of herself but who are nowhere
near what she wants.

She told me that she wants someone exciting and
full of physical and mental energy—an achiever like
herself. She sees herself involved in many adventures
with him. She is also looking for a man with some
sophistication and appreciation for the finer things
in life, probably in his late 30's to early 40's.

I think Sylvia could have some fun with her ad or Internet profile. Using humor would eliminate the risk of sounding pretentious. This is a little of what she could try:

EMMA PEEL SEEKS JOHN STEED WITH A LITTLE JAMES BOND THROWN IN. If you can relate to the old Avengers show on TV and see life as an exciting adventure, we should talk—English or German will do. I'm more the Karate-kicking accomplice (black belt) than the languishing Bond-Babe. So if you want a true partner in crime, someone who you'd be proud to show off on the arm of your Armani tuxedo, or to ski off the highest peak in St. Moritz—the martinis are ready, James. Are you? Because after all the high life we'll be ready to escape to our little hideaway and have the family we both very much want.

There is a secret to using the personals that few people ever figure out. Years ago, when I was a devout vegetarian, I responded to an ad in the personals because I saw the word "vegetarian" in the ad. This was back in the days when there were no voice mail systems, so I responded with a letter. When he replied, I found out that I had read his ad incorrectly; he was a *veterinarian,* not a *vegetarian.* But, we decided not to let that detail stand in our way—we dated for a while, even though we did have some heated discussions on whether or not humans were supposed to be carnivores.

The point is people tend to focus on only one or maybe two words in any ad.

> Even if you write a lengthy print ad or Internet profile that includes every detail of who you are and what you want, you will still discover that most of your respondents have paid attention to only one or two key words.

For example, if your headline says you're into backpacking, you will narrow your options to just those people who are interested in your love of backpacking, but not necessarily in anything else that you consider important.

You can see how the tendency to zero in on one word or concept makes it so important to choose the right words. Companies spend millions on developing effective advertising through research, analysis, and test marketing every word, image, and nuance. What you don't say can be as important as what you do say—especially in a tiny ad. Be sure that every word in your ad is a word you want people to key into—don't say "redhead" unless it doesn't matter to you that people will primarily focus on that attribute.

It is just as important to understand what words will attract attention, as it is to know what words you don't want to dominate attention.

How the Brit Chick Met the Biker Boy

When I was composing the newspaper ad that Robert responded to, I used music as a means to attract the right kind of men. I had figured out by studying ads and talking to many men who were also in the search process that a lot of the men I liked really enjoyed jazz. Instead of just saying "I love jazz" in my ad, I chose to specify a particular composer-performer, Pat Methany, because I thought his music evoked a certain kind of mood for me, and in the mind of the man I was seeking. Then I thought I would add some contrast to that image by saying that I also enjoyed Mozart. This showed my diversity, but more importantly it sent a flag up that the right guy would recognize himself in this music preference and identify himself as a more cultured kind of person. At that time I was not in San Francisco or New York, but living in Southern California where interest in classical music takes a back seat to sports activities. Robert got the message from the word "Mozart" and it influenced him to listen to my voice mail message, which closed the deal, as they say.

Remember that an ad or profile is just a mechanism for grabbing attention; it is a call to action aimed at getting responses from the most broadly qualified people, who will recognize themselves in your words.

You do not have to tell your whole life story. Save that for when you are talking to someone whom you want to know everything about you. A little mystery at first is always more intriguing.

Online Matchmaking

Before we discuss online matchmaking, I want to explain why Internet chat rooms have not been included in this section. Chat rooms are not the smartest or safest way to meet people for two reasons:

A. If you are lonely and isolated, you can get too comfortable with the false sense of intimacy generated by using chat rooms. Some people report getting addicted to them and losing their drive to meet people in person.

B. Chat rooms, despite all the best intentions, are an easy place for unsavory people to prowl the net for potential victims.

Online matchmaking has become a very popular method for people to find each other. Many of the things we discussed in print romance ads apply to the use of online matchmaking services. But with online matchmaking, you can cast a broader net. You may live in a small community miles away from a large town or city that can not provide enough dating prospects for you. You may decide to meet someone through the Internet and maintain a phone and e-mail relationship until you meet in person, then potentially consider moving closer to each other. My husband and I met a happy couple in Mendocino, California, who met online. One person was from the East Coast, the other from California. They met briefly, decided it was right, gave up their jobs, and moved to Mendocino together to open a bookstore there. Another, less happy story concerns a male friend of mine who met a woman online. They corresponded by e-mail for a while, traveled to see each other several times, then decided to move in with each other, across the state at her home in Southern California. It didn't work out, and just months later he found himself with someone whom he liked but couldn't live with, in a place he didn't want to be. If you are considering changing your life radically by moving to be close to someone or to marry them, it is even more important that you attract the most qualified people and screen them rigorously.

1. Cost: Minimal, around $10 to $15 per month to join. Some sites allow you to try their service for thirty days at no cost.

2. Demographics and Competition: To investigate who is using a web site, look through the posted online profiles. Web sites can be very specialized. There are web sites that specialize in astrological matches, animal lovers, gender preference, religious affiliation, and various cultural interests. If the web site itself isn't specialized, look for a way to use its search engine to fine-tune how you scan profiles, and learn what information to include in your profile so it will be transmitted to the appropriate people. Some sites use your key words to scan profiles for you. When a match is found, the search engine automatically sends an e-mail, indicating where you can find the selected profile(s).

3. Preview and References: There are good and bad web sites. Talk to other people you know about their experiences. Keep in mind also that people can easily disguise their age or even gender when using the Internet.

4. Comfort and Convenience: As with print romance ads, you can't see the real person online even if you can see a photo. People have been known to use a picture of themselves when they were younger, or a picture of someone else. Years ago this happened to me. I received a photo of a man who seemed fairly attractive. It came to the time for us to meet. A huge bouquet of roses was strategically delivered seconds before he arrived. When I opened the door, there stood a man with a Prince Valiant haircut and a gleaming gold tooth, wearing a lime green golf shirt stretched over a ten-month "pregnant" belly. The name was the same. The voice was similar. But this was definitely *not* the man in the picture. Clutching the roses, I rushed in to ask my roommate for advice. She was too convulsed in laughter to help. Peering through the thick veil of his cigar smoke later that *long* evening, I found myself still trying to find any resemblance between my date and the man in the photo—was this a case of stolen identity?

Until you hear a voice on the phone, you won't know a person's real gender or age range. Don't waste a great deal of time building e-mail relationships before you have some verbal contact. Be aware that this medium attracts game players and people in transition. To protect your identity, you may choose to get a voice mail service that will allow you to receive messages and hear your respondents' voices, before divulging your personal phone number.

5. Time Invested: It is easy to invest a great deal of time scanning web sites, e-mailing people, calling them, and then meeting them. Remember, screen profiles rigorously, and if you think there is potential, establish voice contact sooner rather than later.

6. Duration: The lack of financial investment reduces the need for a real commitment to the process. There are a wide variety of people using online dating for an equally wide range of reasons. Consequently, it can take quite a lot of time to sift through the masses to meet enough quality people.

On the other hand, if you have been out of circulation for a while, this is a user-friendly, low cost method to ease you back into the mainstream. Maintain a sense of humor and a healthy dose of skepticism and you will learn a great deal from all the people you talk to and meet.

Tips for Online Matchmaking

■ Be clear on your dating goal. Seek sites that designate specific intentions, e.g., long-term relationships, just friends, etc. But also recognize that not everybody realizes their true intentions until they get to know someone. Robert was convinced he was not looking for a marriage partner before he met and got to know me.

■ If you have a strong passion in life, consider targeting people who share that passion by using appropriate key words in the site's profile search engine (e.g., animal rescue, stand-up comedy, or archeology).

■ Consider getting voice mail service from your telephone company. Ask for a unique voice mail number. Use this phone number in your e-mail for first contact.

   ■ This allows you to make contact without giving out your home or business number or having to call them when they may learn your phone number through Caller ID.

   ■ By recording a greeting you provide additional screening as well as let potential dates hear your voice.

   ■ Most importantly, their voice response will activate your instincts and help you determine if you want to know more about this person. It will also help you avoid wasting time with someone who is obviously misrepresenting him or herself.

Tips for Voice Mail Messages— Screening and Responses

Once you have developed a print romance ad or Internet profile that generates the kind of response you want, you need to take the next step: screening your responses or responding to someone else's ad or profile. It is important that you hear each other's voice and listen to your instincts. The best way to do this is by using voice mail and the phone. Use your voice mail message to do some of the sorting for you and attract the kind of people you defined in your Meant2Be Profile (and screen out the others).

■ Your message will be most effective if it focuses on the other person—not just what you want to say about yourself.

> You want the right kind of people to recognize themselves in your message.

Let's say David has determined that he is happiest when he is with an individualistic and articulate woman who is comfortable sharing strong opinions and has a dry sense of humor. David needs to work this into his message in such a way that this kind of woman will instantly recognize that David would appreciate these qualities in her.

A Message that Would Work for David:

Hi, my name is David. I guess you could say that I'm kind of like Humphrey Bogart's kid brother. I'm adventurous and romantic, but I've got more hair, talk better, and drink a lot less than Bogey did. I'm looking for my Lauren Bacall. Maybe that's you? You know—a strong minded, witty, one-of-a-kind woman who has her own opinions and likes to discuss them. We may not always agree, but we'll be able to laugh with each other.

■ Make bullet points to remind yourself of what you want to say before you record a voice mail message and before you return a phone call.

■ Do not read from a script since it will sound like a canned speech. Speak at a relaxed pace and smile while you're talking so a smile will come through in your voice.

■ If you're responding to someone's ad be sure you make a reference to what they wrote in their ad—a phrase, a word, something that lets them know you did not just call lots of ads and leave the same message for everyone. People need to know that you are responding because you are interested in *them*.

■ This person may be screening many responses, so you need to say enough to convey a sense of who you are. When you respond to someone else's ad and leave a very brief message such as "Hi, this is Joan. I saw your ad in the paper, you can call me at 555-1234," it is unlikely that you will get a response. Why should someone return your call when you didn't tell them anything about yourself?

■ Don't talk too long or go into too much detail when recording or leaving a message. It's a matter of balance; your objective is to motivate someone to call you back. Later, when you are talking to each other on the phone, you can learn enough about each other to decide if you want to meet. You might want to leave a message like this:

> Hi, my name's Joan. I really liked your comment about cats being the best company. It sounds like we're both independent types and might have some other things in common too, like going to independent movies. And I like a man with a sense of humor like yours. I would like it if you would call me at my voice mail number, 555-1234, and leave me a message telling me a bit more about yourself and what you're looking for.

■ I always found it helpful to keep notes on people who called, jotting down the key points they made and my impressions of how they sounded. This helped me when I called them back. Most importantly, it helped me to decide if I really wanted to meet them. Likewise, when I received calls, I found myself turned off by people who didn't say anything about my ad or my response.

Video Dating Clubs

Is video dating for you? A romance ad lets you reach a large, broad group of singles very inexpensively, but what if you still prefer seeing whom you are going to meet? What if you are considered attractive and articulate and it's important that you should be seen too?

1. Cost: There can be a significant financial investment required, often a thousand dollars or more, to join a video dating club. And there are often hidden costs, such as having to pay the club photographer to take photos of you to be put in their photo library. This is a very visually competitive medium, so you will want to look your best. This could mean the cost of hair and makeup experts and a special wardrobe. Membership fees can vary significantly, even at the same place. Be sure to read "Getting the Best Deal at Video Dating Clubs" on page 154 before signing any membership agreement.

2. Demographics and Competition: Find out how many men or women who are "active" members of the club meet your basic criteria. Active members are people who are available to date *now* (members "on hold" are out of circulation).

One of our seminar students said he joined a particular video dating club because they promised he would meet lots of women who would meet his basic criteria. He neglected to ask how many other men in the club were like him and would be in competition for these same women. After he joined he found he had too much competition. Consequently, his experience with this club was very disappointing. Whatever your criteria, keep in mind that the most attractive people and higher echelon achievers at video dating clubs tend to be the most popular and therefore the most difficult to date.

3. Preview and References: Just because there are books of attractive people for you to preview doesn't mean these people are all available. As discussed under "Demographics and Competition," many of these people may have their membership on hold because they're exclusively dating one person. The best way to judge the club is to attend special events as a guest and talk to members.

4. Comfort and Convenience: The two most important questions to ask yourself: "Am I comfortable being videotaped?" and "Do I come across well on videotape?" If you answer no to either, then don't waste your money. That doesn't mean you necessarily have to be very good looking, but you had better have the right personality and physical presence needed to compete on tape.

5. Time Invested: Video dating can be a more efficient process than romance print ads. People find video dating clubs convenient because you can walk in, look up a profile, view a video, and place a request. You also get to review the video of anyone that has chosen you and then decide if you want to call them back. Of course, if you're the person initiating contact, you still have to wait for the other person to decide if they are interested. Hearing and seeing people on video can offer a high comfort level, but not everybody looks the same in person as in their photo or video—some people are much more photogenic than others. Some people appear taller or heavier on video than they actually are. In a video dating club environment it's so easy to be primarily affected by how a person looks. It's certainly natural to want to find someone who is physically appealing. But to meet your right kind of person, you need to balance your visual interests with all the other aspects that are going to make you happy, the aspects you have identified in your EMOTIONAL-SNAPSHOT.

6. Duration: The more time you spend reviewing videos and meeting people, the sooner you are likely to meet the right one. Some video dating clubs also include social events for their members and guests. If you like parties, this can expand the number of people you meet through the service and potentially reduce the amount of time it takes you to meet your special person.

Getting the Best Deal at Video Dating Clubs

When you first see a video dating club library you can feel like a kid in a candy store. Imagine shelves bursting with books that are filled with pages of pictures of potential dates! All the more reason you need to ask the right questions when you're considering using a video dating service.

Ask for their membership rates, fees, terms and conditions *in writing*. This should include the cost of renewing your membership. Second, ask if their salespeople are on commission. If the salespeople are on commission and can offer you a better deal, then it's to your advantage to hold out as long as possible while negotiating. Tell them how much you would like to join, but express concern over the price and insist on taking one or more days to think it over. Even though you may lose the "special of the day" by delaying a yes, you will almost always end up with a much lower membership fee.

Negotiating your price is a technique you should also use with other dating services, such as special-interest and dining clubs, that might have commission-based salespeople.

Matchmakers/Introduction Services

Hello Dolly! Like Dolly Levi, from the Broadway play, the old image of the matchmaker was that of a respected, wise, socially well-connected person whose clientele was very select. Today, anybody can hang up a shingle, call themselves a matchmaker, and work for any number of people.

If you are a busy professional, a more introverted person, or just someone who doesn't meet many people in your business and social life, you may want to consider using the services of a professional matchmaker. The concept of having someone find people for you, screen them, and bring that special one to you can be very attractive.

Matchmaking services vary from dating clubs, where they simply provide the venue for you to choose from their membership, to very sophisticated introduction services that can scan the globe, do investigative searches, and use psychological testing to confirm compatibility. Matchmakers may also specialize in specific religions, economic groups, and gender preferences.

1. Cost: You can spend from hundreds to literally ten thousand dollars and more for matchmaking services. Do not under any circumstances be persuaded to waste your matches on people who you feel do not resonate to you, or who do not come close to the type of person you have identified through your Meant2Be Profile.

You need the matchmaker to provide you with enough information about a potential date to get some feelings about this person. Consider your cost per date by dividing the number of introductions you are promised by the cost of your membership. If your membership fee is $500 and you receive a minimum of five introductions, then each date may cost you $100. Is it worth that much to meet someone who is the right height and plays your favorite sport but meets none of your more important criteria? You should also be aware that some matchmakers have a "return policy." If the introduction is totally wrong for you based on what you told the matchmaker, they may not count it against your limited number of introductions. Ask about their return policy before you use their service.

2. Demographics and Competition: Ask the matchmaker how high a priority is given to attracting the type of people who meet your general criteria. Ask them how they market their services to such people. If they say that attracting people who meet your criteria is a high priority, then verify that their clients include a high percentage of these people. If you want to meet men who are 30 to 40 and the matchmaker says they don't have many men right now in that age range, but they are always advertising for them, do you want to pay and then wait until someone answers their advertisement? And, if you are looking for women between 25 and 32, your matchmaker won't be the only one trying to attract them. Women in this age group are the most sought after by matchmakers, because they're considered to be in their prime childbearing years.

We've been concentrating on what *you* are looking for. But don't forget that matchmakers are in a way like job recruiters—they are looking for people who will meet the specific needs of their overall market. For example, they may have a limited number of 25- to 32-year-old women and an excess of 25- to 45-year-old men like you, men who want to meet those popular women. Unless you truly stand out, why would you want to be their client? If they take you on as a client, you will have lots of competition for the few 25- to 32-year-old women, who are probably already having a ball meeting loads of men. And what if matchmakers consider you to be of an age group or physical appearance that is not desirable in terms of their target customers? Some matchmakers turned me down, sight unseen, because I was over 40. Their brutal honesty at least revealed their limitations before I spent money where I would not have received adequate attention.

Compare the various strategies used by different matchmakers to attract the kind of people you want to meet. Find a matchmaker who will represent you willingly and positively, whatever your age or appearance. As long as you show pride in yourself and your appearance, these characteristics do not have to be disqualifiers.

If introduction services don't welcome your patronage, keep in mind that there are other ways for you to meet people. Don't let other people's judgment of you, based on their limited thinking, get in the way of your realizing that you are a wonderful person. There is someone out there who will appreciate who you are, just the way you are.

3. Preview and References: It is best if you are able to independently seek out people who have used a particular matchmaking service. References from the business itself may be less than impartial; you may be referred only to personal friends or clients who have received special treatment. As with any dating service, start by checking with the Better Business Bureau and other agencies to find out if there are complaints on file against the organization (or matchmaker). And, as with video dating and special-interest clubs, make sure their standard rates, refund policies, and performance measurements are in writing—that is, how much does it cost for how many matches over what time period, and how you can cancel your membership if they fail to fulfill their part of the agreement. As with any dating service, you don't want to work with a service whose representatives change their tune with everyone they sign up.

With legitimate matchmakers, using their success rate— that is, how many of their introductions have culminated in marriage—may not be the ideal measure of their talents. People generally have difficulty figuring out what will make them happy in a relationship. It's unrealistic to expect a stranger to do that for you. Even if more than a few marriages have happened within a matchmaker's membership, it may have been a matter of luck, not skill. Nevertheless, some matchmakers are skilled in reading people and using both their analytical and intuitive skills to bring the right people together. Finding and recognizing gifted matchmakers is the challenge.

4. Comfort and Convenience: Ask yourself how comfortable you are with the people who interview you. Ask if they will be the one making the matches; if not, make sure you talk to the matchmaker. Tune out the sales pitch and listen to your instincts. Does the person interviewing or matchmaking fit your style? Because many introduction services say their membership includes the best looking, most successful, etc., try to determine if they are overselling themselves. Are they being realistic? Ask about their infrastructure: What staff and technological support do they have to serve clients? A less expensive, one-person shop with a large client base may find it difficult, if not impossible, to respond to individual phone calls. If the matchmaker uses compatibility surveys that focus on general criteria and common interests, be aware that while this is OK for basic screening, these kinds of surveys are no basis for true *compatibility*. If the matchmaker is going to be effective, he or she must focus on your needs, as defined in your Meant2Be Profile. In fairness to matchmakers, I think we tend to put ourselves passively in their hands and expect them to wave a magic wand and bring us Mr. or Ms. Perfect. It's up to you to inform them who that person is for you.

> You need to see a matchmaker as your agent, someone who goes out and spreads the word for you. But you have to be clear about what you're looking for in order for this type of partnership to be effective.

5. Time Invested: After your initial meeting and interview(s) with the matchmaker, all you have to do is wait for them to supply you with candidates to meet.

6. Duration: It could take a while for the matchmaker to find you enough truly qualified candidates, unless you are lucky enough to be in great demand within the matchmaker's membership. Even if you are in this position, you need to make sure these are people *you* want to meet.

Deciding Whom You Want to Meet and Where

How do you decide whom you want to call and whom you want to go out with if you haven't seen each other? *Listen to your instincts.*

Most of us are affected by how a person sounds. How does that voice make you feel? Does the person sound impatient and defensive, or relaxed, warm, and open? Listen to the tone of their voice, not just the words.

It is important to talk, then meet, before developing an intensive e-mail relationship. You may be charmed by someone's wit on paper or e-mail only to be disappointed by the way they come across on the phone and in person.

Start with a clear understanding of what you want. Is your goal just to meet more people, date casually, and have some fun, or is it to find a long-term, committed relationship? Be clear about your intent. Likewise, don't underestimate the importance of understanding the intent of the other person.

Save your intent for voice mail. Placing it in the written ad may narrow the field of potential respondents too much. Many people are not comfortable being viewed from the outset as serious relationship material. Robert wasn't looking for a wife when he responded to my ad. I had not indicated my intentions. When we talked, however, I was able to discern he was serious about wanting one special person in his life.

161

Remember, *you* are the one who decides who you will meet. You can choose *not* to meet anyone. You have no obligation to put yourself in any situation where you don't feel safe and comfortable, or where you simply won't enjoy yourself. As I mentioned earlier, meeting men in daylight was important to me; consequently, any time I met someone in a dark restaurant or bar we never clicked—and we often clashed, quite possibly because I wasn't comfortable in that environment.

> You are in the driver's seat, even if you responded to someone else's ad, profile, or video, or were brought together through a matchmaker. You decide what makes you comfortable, who you want to meet, and where you want to meet them.

Don't meet too many people in the same place. I met so many men at the same neighborhood restaurant that the waiters started winking at me, because they thought I was in a certain kind of business!

Decide where you feel most comfortable. Maybe you prefer dressing up and being in upscale surroundings when you meet people. A person you're going to meet prefers just getting together after working out at the gym. Although this person meets many of your basic criteria, will you feel your best if you meet them dressed this casually?

If you have to change your style of dress, the venue you prefer, or anything else just to please or be compatible with someone else, that is not a good sign. Your goal is to find someone with whom you are comfortable just being yourself.

It's OK to say to someone that the place they want to meet isn't your cup of tea. Maybe you can find some other common ground. But if you can't, or you're just not comfortable, move on. Better to find out now than later. Why spend time meeting someone who makes you feel uncomfortable?

Activity and Special-Interest Clubs

There are literally hundreds of varieties of special-interest clubs. Consequently, this section can not discuss how each of the categories in the Meant2Be Dating Resource Evaluator applies to each type of special-interest club. Instead, what you will find are broad guidelines to help you evaluate the potential of special-interest clubs. Contract negotiations with special-interest clubs should follow the same rules as outlined in the "Video Dating" and "Matchmaking" sections.

To decide if activity or special-interest clubs are for you, first ask yourself two questions:

A. Do I like group activities, or do I prefer meeting one-on-one?

B. If I make friends but don't meet that special person, will I still feel that my time and money were well spent?

> Do not join a club just to find that special someone who shares your particular interest.

Having interests in common is *not* a prerequisite for *compatibility*. You are looking for someone who shares your style—someone who is simpatico with your interests, someone who understands *why* white water rafting is such a thrill—but not necessarily someone who has or will actively participate in your particular interest. When you shop for a special-interest or activity club, think about why you are joining. If you are joining a tennis club just to find people to play tennis with, that's fine. But if finding someone who is creative is more important to you than finding a tennis buddy, then you should consider joining a club that primarily attracts creative people. There, you are more likely to find your someone special, someone who is both creative *and* active, someone who will appreciate your love of tennis, even if they don't themselves play tennis.

> The primary reason for joining a special-interest club is to be in an environment where you enjoy yourself, feel confident, and are at ease.

Couples who have met though activity clubs say these connections rarely occurred as a result of events organized around their special interests. Instead, they got to know each other during an all-day club event where they were there just to have fun with a group of other people. It wasn't hiking or sailing that magically brought these couples together; the particular activity had nothing to do with it. Relaxed atmosphere and group camaraderie create the right environment for people to discover the *compatibility* and chemistry that's naturally there.

Lunch and Dining Clubs

Many of our students who are busy professionals like the concept of meeting people in a dining setting. This setting might work for you if you can answer yes to these three questions:

A. Do you consider yourself a good conversationalist with a pleasant manner and a sense of humor?

B. Do you enjoy talking with people about a variety of subjects?

C. Do you have the wardrobe and etiquette needed to make the right impression on dining dates?

Dining clubs generally fall into one of two categories. One type functions strictly as an event organizer where any member can attend. These parallel the activity clubs. The other type uses specific criteria to match people for small group lunches and dinners. These are in some ways similar to matchmakers.

1. Cost: Membership fees can vary from about $100 to $500 or more. Expect additional charges for meals and any special events, etc. Some have no sign-up fees and only charge you the cost of each event.

The open membership type may initially sound like a better deal if cost is a consideration. Remember though that you are paying for the opportunity to have an intimate meal with people you can enjoy, people with whom you have some basis for *compatibility*. What is the dining club's basis for matching? It's important to know this as you factor the cost.

2. Demographics and Competition: The clubs that match couples for lunch, or small groups for dinner, require much more research on your part to determine their demographics and your competition. You want to know what their criteria are for matching you. If it's mainly by age and interests, is this worth the cost? If you do not fall into the "average" category in terms of your height, weight, or appearance, find out how they factor these differences into their "matchmaking." It is not enough for them just to say they will. Ask them how many of their members are like you, unless you are comfortable standing out from the other guests at each dinner.

3. Preview and References: When you are interviewing the club before joining, ask the hard questions. How often will you be matched for meals? How is your input on the suitability of those matches addressed? How many lunches or dinners do they guarantee you will be invited to during the term of your membership contract? Is this a realistic number based on the size of their membership? Where do you fit within their membership demographics? If you are older or larger than their typical member, this may affect how often you will be matched.

If the club seems like a good possibility, ask if you can attend a social event as a guest. Talk to the people there to determine if you'll meet people there who might fit your basic criteria and resonate with your EMOTIONAL-SNAPSHOT.

4. Comfort and Convenience: Do you prefer small groups and one-on-one conversations to large parties? Are you more comfortable with a casual lunch or a carefully orchestrated dinner? Do you enjoy and contribute to stimulating table conversations? Will you be required to sit with just the people they choose or will you be able to meet other members?

5. Time Invested: If all you have to do is show up, then your time requirement is very low.

6. Duration: If you have to wait until they find or arrange suitable matches for meals, then depending on their matchmaking skills, it may take some time to meet enough people to be able to choose the right one. Some dining clubs help fill in the gaps between dining parties by offering general group social events for members to meet one another on their own.

In Summary

I hope you can see how important it is to research every dating service in which you consider investing your time, money, and emotional energy to meet people. Put aside the insecurities and the loneliness. *Put on your business hat.* Use the Dating Resource Evaluator to assess each dating service and resource based on all the factors we have outlined for you. Then get out there, the confident you with the EMOTIONAL-SNAPSHOT of how you want to feel with your right one tucked away in your "pocket". Dating will be more fun, more interesting, and more relaxed because you'll know you are going to meet the right one for you.

Dating Advice—*"AskPhilippa"*
Answers to Real-Life Dating Challenges

Dating Advice—*"AskPhilippa"*

Answers to Real-Life Dating Challenges

This chapter includes answers to composites of letters from actual readers of *"AskPhilippa"*, my online dating advice column for single adults. Names and locations have been changed to ensure privacy. Topics include using romance print ads, joining a special-interest club, dating single parents, getting back into the dating scene, trying to date unavailable people, finding men who like 40-plus women, carrying a torch for a past lover, the Odd Couple syndrome, online dating, taking a vacation together, bad timing, and getting beyond short-term relationships.

These letters were selected because they deal with many of the issues single adults are faced with today.

It Pays to Advertise

Dear Philippa:

I really get a kick out of reading the romance print ads. Someone at work met their boyfriend this way, but I don't know if I have the nerve to try it. I have a thing about artists. Can I meet them this way? Is it safe to meet people this way? What do you think?

—Suzy, Sunnyvale, California

Dear Suzy:

If your concern about using the romance print ads is safety, I don't think that you are at any greater risk meeting someone from the personals at a well-populated place, than you are meeting someone at a party or singles event. However, I think it is a good idea to be cautious about whatever dating activity you choose.

Placing your own ad is the best way to protect your identity. With the right ad, you can attract just the kind of person you are looking for—not just fit into someone else's selection process. You need to ask yourself what your intent is for using the romance print ads—to date more? Find one special person? Get married? Don't limit the number of responses to your ad by including strong intentions. Save it for the voice mail message if it is really important to you. Not everyone knows they're ready for a serious relationship before they meet the right person.

Remember, romance print ads are advertising. Following basic advertising principals will get the kind of responses you want.

Find a way to get attention and differentiate yourself from all the other ads. Don't use a similar headline. What sets you apart? What do people find interesting about you? Say what you have to say concisely. Limit yourself to just one or two key thoughts. Save your qualifying information for the voice mail message. Remember, the personal ad is just a mechanism for grabbing attention and influencing the most broadly qualified people to call your mailbox.

You said you liked artistic types, so you might try something like:

> **FIND ME AT GALLERY OPENINGS.** I'll be the tall brunette with the mischievous smile admiring your talents. You'll be the (age range), tall slim, smiling man who's ready for the right woman to inspire his future.

Notice how you get attention by immediately saying something artistic guys can relate to: galleries. Then you intrigued the guy with a little physical description. Finally, you appealed to his creative ambitions and romantic dreams.

Suzy, you need to figure out what kind of person you want to meet—the qualities and traits that are most important to you—and work it into your voice mail message, not just saying what you want but focusing on the other person. Be "you" oriented; it's more appealing. In your case, you might talk about how you find yourself most comfortable with artistic men because you enjoy their openness to new ideas and experiences. This way you've told them that you are adventuresome, too, but you stated it from their point of view.

Good luck, Suzy. Find yourself a masterpiece.

Reaching Your Peak

Dear Philippa:

I've been thinking about joining a singles adventure club to meet someone. Do you think this is a good way to find a special woman to date? I love rock climbing and rollerblading and it would be great to have someone to share this with.

—Rocky, San Francisco, California

Dear Rocky:

It sounds like you would have a lot in common with the members of an adventure club, and that it would be a good way to meet people who share your favorite pastimes. If your primary reason for joining is to meet a special woman, not just friends, you need to weigh the costs of joining the club against the opportunities for meeting the kind of women you're looking for. See if you can attend the club as a guest and find out for yourself if there are women in this club who might fit your criteria. If this isn't possible, ask for the names and numbers of three club members and then call them— ask them to describe the types and mix of people they have been meeting at club functions.

Define the other qualities and interests you want a woman to have—you're probably going to do more than just rock climbing and rollerblading in your relationship. You may want to find someone who appreciates the experience and rush you get from your activities, not necessarily someone with just your rock climbing or rollerblading experience. You might also want to broaden your scope to include women who want to be introduced to your interests while you learn theirs. Remember, having specific interests in common is not the basis for overall compatibility. You probably want to meet someone who will share all of life's adventures, not be just a rollerblading and rock climbing buddy of the opposite sex. I think you are on the right track by trying to meet people at places where you can just be yourself. Compare the club you're looking at to other venues for the likelihood of meeting a special woman. Rocky, listen to your instincts—you'll know what feels right.

Happy adventures, Rocky.

When the Mating Game Becomes the Waiting Game

Dear Philippa:

I keep meeting men who I am very interested in, and they seem very interested in me. But, between their work and children, these men are too busy to give me all the time I would like to talk and keep in touch. This makes me anxious because I don't feel like I can call them. What can I do?

—Jennie, Palo Alto, California

Dear Jennie:

Why do we always seem to pursue the ones who can't give us what we need? Then we turn ourselves into pretzels trying to be the kind of person who fits into someone else's lifestyle. No wonder we feel anxious and off balance. It's time for you to step back, take a deep breath, and do something radical.

Start thinking about what you want in someone for a change. What qualities in someone make you happiest? Sounds like the first thing on your list is someone who keeps in touch and makes you feel like you are an important part of their life. There are men out there who are naturally that way. And, when all the other parts of the compatibility and chemistry puzzle fit, they would love talking to and being with you. Don't waste your energy trying to change yourself or anyone else.

Each of us needs to find someone who is in sync with our style. Start believing that you deserve someone in your life who likes keeping in touch with you and who makes you a priority. Once you can clearly imagine how it feels to have this person in your life, you'll start finding these men almost literally coming out of the woodwork. Define what other aspects of someone are important to you, so you can have these other compatibility factors clearly in your mind as you meet people.

Keep in mind that what one person calls needy, another person calls being close.

Jennie, you just have to find the right person for you.

Back in the Dating Game

Dear Philippa:

My wife and I broke up after 10 years. She left about five months ago. I'm lonely and I just don't feel that I have what it takes to attract anybody. My sister says my problem is poor self-esteem. What can I do to change the way women see me and attract the right kind of women?

—Joe, Mendocino, California

Dear Joe:

After a relationship ends the readjustment can be painful, especially when we are left behind. Give yourself time to heal. There are many excellent books on increasing self-esteem and dealing with loss, in the self-help section of your neighborhood bookstore, that can help you get back on your feet.

Our divorced students say that after using the Meant2Be Profile to define the kind of person with whom they will feel the happiest, they realize why their marriages didn't work. Often long-term relationships end because of poor compatibility. When you identify the style, traits, and values in a person that you need to be happy, this may free you from a sense of failure. You will also realize that you can have someone in your life who accepts you just the way you are— someone who can be a true life partner and friend, as well as lover. This may well fill you with renewed hope.

I will let you know how to obtain more information about this Profile and how to use dating resources effectively to meet the right people. So, when you are ready to venture out again, this time you will feel prepared to recognize a woman with whom you have compatibility as well as chemistry.

Joe, it may be difficult for you to believe right now, but there is a woman looking for someone just like you. You just need to know how to recognize her.

When Love is a One-Way Street

Dear Philippa:

I met a girl this past summer, and although we only spoke twice, I really liked her. I saw her around, but I didn't ask her out until the fall. I complimented her looks and told her she had a cool personality. But, she said no to dating me because she had lots of boyfriends. I even asked if I could change anything about myself, like my personality, but she said I should join a club or something to meet girls. This has happened to me four times. I still like that girl and she smiles at me. My friends told me to move on…there are more fish in the sea. I might send her a Valentine card or ask her out again. What should I do?

—Brian, Southfield, Michigan

Dear Brian:

I know just how you feel. Why is it that the people we like are often not available? That is a hard lesson to learn at any age. But, what really concerns me is that you feel you might need to change your personality to get this girl's interest. One of the keys to real happiness in any relationship is having someone in your life who likes you just the way you are. You shouldn't have to change yourself to have someone like you. And, while persistence can be an admirable trait, you have to learn to be flexible and to know when to let go. Letting go is easier when you realize that you are not giving away your one and only chance. Have the confidence to say goodbye to the wrong one so you can meet the right ones. I said right ones, Brian, because there will always be more than one person out there who is right for you. Your friends are right—it is time to move on.

Try paying more attention to girls who seem to like you— girls who laugh at your jokes and ask you questions about yourself. Try placing your attention and interest where there seems to be some reciprocal interest. Sometimes, someone you just thought of as just a casual friend can become a very special someone in your life.

Stay true to yourself, Brian, and remember that dating is supposed to be fun—not hard work.

Where Are All the Good Guys?

Dear Philippa:

I am a divorced woman in my forties who finds it difficult to meet men who are like me—mature, educated, professional, and energetic. I prefer not to date men I work with; and, while I go to church, grocery stores, the beach, I do not seem to find men who are interested in meeting me. Can you tell me where else to look?

—Marie, Miami, Florida

Dear Marie:

Sometimes, when we reach a certain age, we develop a belief system that there are fewer people out there who could be interested in us. Yes, the number of available people may be fewer when we are older. But, whatever age you are, all you need is the right one— not large numbers.

I am frequently asked where the best places to meet people are, by men and women of all ages (and preferences). The simple answer is that the best place to meet someone is where you feel the most comfortable. You need to just be yourself, because that is where the true you will shine. You want to ultimately connect with that special someone who will like you just the way you are.

The not-so-simple answer is that everyone has a different interpretation of what method of meeting people is the most comfortable. Some people thrive on small group conversation, and like dressing up and meeting people through dining clubs. Some have the looks and/or confidence to enjoy video dating. And others, who like the camaraderie of group activities, prefer meeting people through adventure or special-interest activity clubs.

In our Meant2Be classes we use a simple matrix to help each person evaluate and select the right method for meeting people. Here is a simple way to get started: First make a list of your options—methods for meeting people—both ones you have tried and new possibilities. Rate each of these options, based on your comfort, the cost, the time involved, and the number of men that you think you would meet who fit your basic criteria (e.g., age, religion). It is best if you choose to use several different methods concurrently to meet people. For instance, it would not be advisable to depend on just a matchmaker to provide all your social connections, due to the extended amount of time it could take to meet just a few people.

If you have been out of the dating scene for a while, you may want to gear up and gain some confidence before trying new methods of meeting people. Some people find newspaper or Internet ads easier at first, because they allow anonymity until a comfort level is reached. It is important that you consider everyone you meet as simply an opportunity to clarify what you are looking for in that special someone. Practice saying no thanks to the wrong ones (they may say no thanks to you too). This way you will be ready to recognize and say yes to the right one when he comes along.

Old Lovers Are Like Boomerangs

Dear Philippa:

A long time ago I was involved with a wonderful man, but, unfortunately, I ended the relationship. I never married and often regretted my mistake. He married but has been divorced for several years. Recently I got back in touch with him and we started seeing each other again. I try not to call him between dates, but other than great sex, we hardly keep in touch, and he doesn't show any signs of being interested in more than just a physical relationship. Do you think he still needs time to get over his divorce, or am I wasting my time?

—Terri, Boston, Massachusetts

Dear Terri:

Have you been carrying a torch for him all these years? Have you blocked other relationship possibilities in hopes that your dream of getting back together again with him would eventually come true?

Many people look back nostalgically on past relationships. Sometimes when we are feeling lonely, or facing something such as attending a friend's wedding or spending the Christmas holidays alone, it makes us want to try to recapture a happier time with someone we used to know. The sad truth is that the reality of seeing this person again rarely lives up to our imagination. The other person is just not in the same mind-set we are in. They may have some fond memories, but emotionally they have often moved on.

Terri, it is time for you to also move on. Distinguish your dream from reality; focus on what you really want and need in a relationship, rather than what this man does or does not want. You deserve to have someone in your life who is equally invested in the relationship and has the same level of admiration and affection for you as you have for him. Imagine having a genie that could materialize the ideal man for you. What is he like? What is your life together like? This is not a dream from the past. This is a reality just waiting to happen. Let go of the past, and make room in your life for this wonderful man to appear. And he will.

Sweet Smells of Romance

Dear Philippa:

I was dating a great woman for a month or so, taking things slowly after both our divorces. We both wanted to be sure we really liked each other before getting physical, so we waited and planned a romantic dinner at her place. I had never been in her house before. We had always met at restaurants and other places so we wouldn't be tempted to go further than we were ready to go. Everything seemed perfect until I saw her place and how she lived. She had a parrot that flew free around her place and it wasn't house trained. I think she never even changed her sheets because there were crumbs everywhere. And the bathroom—phew! How can I tell this woman we can't go on seeing each other because she's a slob?

— Ron, Berkeley, California

Dear Ron:

I am sure that once you got past the shock of seeing her place, you were also disappointed that you are obviously incompatible. I'm sorry this happened, but better you found out before getting further involved. Maybe next time you can casually drop by a new woman's place during the day to drop off something and get a glimpse of how she lives before planning the big romantic evening.

189

Your story reminded me of the time I went into someone's bathroom and saw strange green organisms reproducing before my eyes. That can really kill a mood if things like that bother you. Let's face it, we all have different levels of hygiene and housecleaning. Maybe you have to look closer for clues about how a person lives. Notice if their car looks like you need a garden rake to clean it out, or if after a meal there is more food on them than in them.

Now, the hardest part for you is to inform her that the relationship will not work, and to do it without hurting her feelings. You could say you're not ready for this relationship—but this could open up a conversation that you don't want to have. You could tell her that you are such a clean freak that you make Felix Unger of the *Odd Couple* look like a slob, and you know it would drive her crazy (indicating that you are the one with the problem). But with this explanation, you could risk the chance that she would love to have someone like you to bring sweet, Lysol-smelling order into her life. If all else fails, tell her you have a bird phobia. If she has to choose between you and the bird, pray that she chooses the bird.

Chasing Cheerleaders

Dear Philippa:

I'm back dating, after a recent divorce, and I feel like I'm fourteen again by asking this question, but how does a guy know when someone is interested in him? There's this young woman in my condo complex that I like a lot, but I seem to be getting mixed messages from her. I knew she was seeing someone, but it couldn't have been that serious because she's always flirting with me. She invites herself over all the time. She even kissed me. I have bought her little presents and dropped hints about being interested in being more than friends. Then she disappeared with some other guy. Now she has ended that relationship and she's spending time with me. We are still friends but I don't know if I should make a move.

—Paul, Seattle, Washington

Dear Paul:

Trying to figure out someone else's intentions and interest level is always a challenge, no matter what age you are. They don't call it the dating game for nothing.

Start by asking yourself how you feel when you are around this woman. Are you excited? Off balance? Frustrated? Now, imagine yourself with women you're attracted to, with whom you feel relaxed and playful, accepted, women who you never have to guess how they feel about you. Get the picture? Aren't these the kind of relationships you would enjoy experiencing? You seem to spend a lot of energy concentrating on what this one woman does or doesn't want. Ms. Condo sounds like she's enjoying life and having fun. How about figuring out what you really want and then finding someone who wants the same thing?

Be gentle with yourself. Recovering from a divorce takes time. Try and put yourself in situations that are going to reinforce your confidence with positive outcomes. Ms. Condo reminds me of the high school cheerleader the guys always wanted to ask out. So, let her shake her pom-poms, and remember, she's just playing the game.

Online Connection—
Off Line Intimacy

Dear Philippa:

I recently met a man using an Internet match site. We got together and hit it off right away. Even though I'm a big woman, my weight didn't seem to bother him. We went hiking and talked and we even talked about having a future together. Then I found out he was back online trying to meet other women and I was devastated. I wonder if I said something wrong or if my weight really is the problem.

—June, Minneapolis, Minnesota

Dear June:

I totally relate to your experience. I used to feel the same way when I found romance print ads run by someone I was dating. I felt hurt and outraged. But the reality is that when we first date someone, they have the right to meet and date anyone else they like.

I think these feelings have to do with our desire for instant intimacy, especially if we've been alone for a while and tend to over romanticize new relationships. It takes time to get to know someone and decide if they are long-term material. Sometimes when you are in a romantic setting, like sharing a nature hike, you get caught up in the closeness of the moment and you both enjoy imagining future possibilities. This doesn't mean that your date has decided that you are the one, or that you should think that they are the one for you.

Forget the self-criticism. This has nothing to do with you doing something wrong or being the wrong size. There are many reasons why this man may have decided to keep playing the field. It doesn't really matter why he did. All that matters is that you decide what you want. You may decide to date several different people, sharing different interests and activities with each of them, as a way of safeguarding yourself from getting too romantically involved with one person too soon. You may also want to have an open discussion with your dates about each of your dating styles. Let each other know that you'll be meeting different people, so you can discover what you both want in a relationship. This will take the pressure off for both of you.

Also keep in mind that online and personal ad dating are some of the least expensive methods to meet a lot of people. Because of the minimal financial investment, people use this approach to find dates for a variety of reasons: just to have fun, to explore their sexuality, to bounce back from failed relationships, as well as to meet the love of their life.

Be cautious, take it slow, and get to know and like your dates as their true self unfolds over time. The results can pay off big time, as many successful online daters can tell you.

When a Romantic Getaway Turns into a Let Me Get Away

Dear Philippa:

After two years of dating, my boyfriend and I just took our first real vacation together. What we thought would be a romantic getaway turned out very differently than we had hoped. Now my boyfriend says we need to take a break from each other. He is basing the future of our relationship on this bad vacation experience. To be honest, our relationship has always been a bit volatile. When it is very good, it is wonderful, but when it's bad, all we do is fight. We love each other but neither of us knows if the other is "the one." Is my boyfriend right— should we break up?

    —Kelly, Chicago, Illinois

Dear Kelly:

This story reminds me of a time I went away to a cabin in the woods for a romantic weekend with the man I was dating. It turned out he had also invited another couple. His idea of fun was playing cards and just hanging around. I wanted to get out and hike and enjoy nature. The other couple acted like rabbits all weekend, and while we never saw them, we certainly heard them. By the end of the weekend, he and I couldn't wait to get back to our respective homes, *alone.* Why can vacations strain or break relationships? I think this is because the time we spend away together with someone acts like an incubator that heats

195

up any major incompatibilities that already exist in the relationship.

In your case, the vacation was the straw that broke the camel's back. It sounds like maybe it is a matter of your love having grown without the compatibility being there in place first. Ideally, if you could play the tape back and return to the beginning of the relationship, you would take the time to decide if you are really right for each other in terms of overall compatibility before getting deeply enmeshed in love. Your boyfriend sounds like he is facing some harsh realities. This is painful for both of you. If you both really want to try and save your relationship, you may want to consider seeking couples counseling.

My advice would be for both of you to take the time apart to define the kind of person with whom you can be truly happy. Think about your values, goals, and preferred lifestyle. Then come together and try to talk objectively about what each of you want, where the differences are, what things are not negotiable, and what things are. You may have to face the painful truth that your incompatibilities are too great and that loving each other is not enough. I hope this is not the case, but if it is, you need to find the strength to let each other go and find happiness. You each deserve to have someone in your life with whom you have both love and harmony. If it is necessary, be willing to let go of each other, so that you can each find your special person.

The Right Person The Wrong Time

Dear Philippa:

After years of trying, I finally met the woman of my dreams. I felt so safe talking to her. We could talk late into the night telling each other about everything. She appreciated all my attention and returned it. We even had the same life goals. We had one particular magical night together. We even talked about the future together. The next day I was ten feet off the ground in love. I called her and then out of the blue she told me things were happening too fast and we weren't right for each other. I was shocked and devastated. I went over and spoke to her for hours. She kept bringing up her old relationship with the only man she said she's ever loved. She had told me before that he had ended their relationship and she had mentioned seeing him again not long ago. She said she really likes me. But my phone calls and e-mails to her have gone nowhere. It's over. Is there anything I can do to win this wonderful woman back?

—Ken, Omaha, Nebraska

Dear Ken:

It sounds like you fell hard and fast. You were open and ready to love and be loved, and you thought she was too. But unfortunately, it sounds like she wasn't.

It is possible to have most of the pieces of the compatibility puzzle with someone, like your shared intimacy and goals with your lady, Ken, but still be missing that one crucial piece—mutual timing. Sometimes we are blinded by our romantic feelings. The clues are often in fact there long before the person tells us it can't work and the sledgehammer hits us. There is often a part of someone that is held separate from us in some way. We do more of the pursuing, the communicating, and the date planning. The closer we get, the more the other person gets afraid, until the closeness becomes unbearable. This often happens after an incredibly wonderful time together, when you have been closer to someone than you have ever been before.

There are several schools of thought on this subject. You could back off and give her space and see how she resolves her feelings with this other man. This would mean that you stay away from her for a while. Trying to be just friends while this goes on rarely works. You will torture yourself watching her date someone else and end up putting pressure on her, which will drive her away permanently. Think about love as a butterfly that lands on your hand. This beautiful, delicate creature chose to grace your life. As long as you hold your hand out the butterfly can come back. But if you try to grasp the butterfly, you will crush it.

Another of life's ironies is that when you really let this woman go so she can find happiness, and you go on to opening yourself up to loving others, one day she might turn up on your doorstep, when you least expect it. But by then, you may have a deeper love in your life. I can't explain why this is; it just seems to happen that way.

198

You sound like a very loving person Ken. Keep your heart open and have faith. You are going to have someone in your life who is ready to love you. All this painful stuff is the practice we need so we can recognize the right one when they come along.

When Long-Term Relationships Are Measured in Months

Dear Philippa:

I am an attractive, intelligent, 32-year-old woman. I'm independent, work for myself, and own a condo. While I have no trouble meeting men, holding their interest is another matter. I am considered fun to be with by the men I date. The only problem is that I seem to be doing something wrong, because in less than a month the men I am seeing start cooling off and telling me they just want to be friends. Is it me or them?

    —Stacy, Gainesville, Florida

Dear Stacy:

I too used to think that getting beyond a few weeks of dating someone was difficult. My family and friends thought I was on a revolving man-a-month plan. I don't know enough about how you are meeting these men, or why you choose to date certain ones, to be able to talk specifically to your situation. I can, however, offer this insight, based on my personal experience and the stories I hear from the students who attend Meant2Be seminars.

Most of us, when we are dating, believe in the myth: If I could only meet enough people, then eventually the right one will come along. The reality is that if you don't know what you are really looking for in the first place—and that means the right kind of man for you, Stacy—then you will just meet lots of people who are wrong for you. If you are finding dates online, for example, and you get many responses, that can be a great ego boost. The problem with that is that unless you carefully screen all those responses for the right kind of man for you, you will end up spending a great deal of time with men who can be bad news for you.

Another aspect may be that when we are hungry for companionship, we end up giving up our power and become almost grateful when someone reasonably attractive shows interest in us. We stop choosing whom we want to date, based on the right type of person for us. Then when the person who chose us loses interest, we are left wondering why.

You describe yourself as an independent and accomplished woman, Stacy. Are you taking control of your love life by figuring out whom you really want to date and whom you want to spend your time with? Try saying no to the ones who do not really fit your needs. Look beyond the physical attraction and instant charm and ask yourself: Is this the kind of man I can see sharing my life with for the long-term?

Stop thinking that you are doing something wrong, Stacy. When you find the right kind of man for you, he will like you just the way you are. The parts of you that may scare off the wrong ones are the things that the right man will love, or at the very least accept, in you. Start visualizing yourself with the right man—sharing a life together that stretches out far into your future—and you will have him.

I'll be Calling You—
and Other Famous Last Lines

Dear Philippa:

I am a recently divorced woman who is trying to get back out into the world. I have been using the Internet to meet people. The problem is what to do or say to someone who sounded great on the phone, but when you meet them, it's obvious they aren't right. I don't like hurting people's feelings and this all feels so awkward.

—Helen, Toronto, Ont.

Dear Helen:

Besides those first, uncomfortable minutes when you meet someone, I think there is nothing more difficult than knowing what to say when the date is over. I wish we could have thought balloons over our heads like cartoon people. Then we could understand what the other person is thinking: Did the date go well? Do I want to see this person again? Do they want to see me again?

One way to ease this situation is to be realistic before you meet anyone for the first time. First, build a safe getaway into your meeting plans. You might agree to meet for just a quick cup of coffee. Say this to the other person ahead of time, so that when it is time for you to make your exit, they will not think you just want to get away from them. Even if rockets go off when you meet, a planned getaway allows you the option of setting up another date or staying for another cup of coffee.

Second, realize that it does not matter how well you got along together on the phone; there is absolutely no guarantee that this rapport will continue in person. The anonymity of the telephone allows people to let their guard down and reveal themselves—their interests, thoughts, and humor—more easily.

When you meet for the first time you are both understandably uncomfortable, and rapport may seem to go out the window. Sometimes you have to give each other enough time to relax and see if the rapport comes back—this may take more than one meeting. And sometimes when you allow time for rapport to develop, the chemistry may follow.

The change in rapport from the phone to the first meeting often has to do with expectations about looks. Spending a great deal of time imagining what a person looks like is dangerous. Other than each other's basic statistics, it's best to have no specific picture in mind before meeting.

Beware of the person who wants to know every detail about how you look, or whom you look like, before you meet. This kind of person is sure to have some fantasy that can only pale in comparison to the reality. Some people try to get past all this by exchanging pictures before they meet. But people can look very different from their picture—if it is their picture!

What if even after an OK time together you feel strongly that there is no reason to see each other again? Don't wait for the other person to bring it up. Simply say that there is no real connection between you. This is something everyone can understand. Then leave, so you won't be pulled into unpleasant explanations—the other person may well be planning your next date.

What if you clash with someone right after you meet them? What if you find something unpleasant or threatening about them? Leave immediately. Don't tough it out for the full fifteen or twenty minutes. Simply say something like "I'm sorry, but this just isn't working out for me," and then leave as quickly as you can. Your well-being and safety come first. The other person shouldn't be that surprised. Negative chemistry is a two-way situation.

Meeting people online is a great way to reach a large number of prospects. The down side is the extensive screening process. Be discriminating about whom you want to meet. Listen to your instincts and how the voice at the other end of the phone makes you feel. Then be realistic and save the dreaming until you've at least met each other and agreed to go out on another date. All this will help cushion the inevitably uncomfortable "thanks-but-no-thanks."

Meeting the right people online is a numbers game. Keep your sense of humor and remember the numbers are in your favor, Helen. You only need one right person—and that person is looking for you too.

It's Time Baby

Dear Philippa:

You're probably surprised to get this kind of letter from a guy. Well, I'm a 37-year-old divorced male, and I want to meet the right girl and start a family. I meet enough women, but I don't seem to be able to find ones I like and who are interested in starting a family. I love kids and I come from a large Italian family with lots of nieces and nephews. What should I do? I don't want to be a 40-year-old bachelor.

    —Sal, Philadelphia

Dear Sal:

It's not unusual for men around your age to want to settle down and start a family. But the anxiety I detect in your letter concerns me. Have you noticed that when you feel good about yourself, you act relaxed and tend to be more attractive to people? What happens when you are around people who are feeling anxious or needy? You want to run the other way, right?

Imagine that we all have neon signs on us that blink certain messages. Some people's signs say "kick me" or "stay away—I don't trust you." Your sign seems to be saying "I have to find a woman who wants a baby now!" This could be driving away the very women you want to meet.

Your fears of scarcity are creating your negative reality. There are unlimited women out there that you could like, and who are interested in starting a family with the right guy. Remember, you only need to meet one right woman.

To change your mindset, imagine what your life will be like with the woman you are going to meet. See yourself laughing together as you push Sal Jr's stroller. Don't worry about what she looks like. Just enjoy the feeling and start believing this can and will happen.

Instead of watching a family in a restaurant and feeling your heart squeezed with sadness, start to feel excited about what is coming into your life. The most important thing is for you to find a lady with whom you can have a strong, loving relationship. Not everyone knows, when they are dating, that they want to marry—much less start a family. Those types of life decisions emerge over time and through trust.

Now, let's talk specifically about what you can do to put yourself in touch with women who are ready to start a family. How about looking close at hand, like at a place of worship? Or you could try online dating and include in your profile how important family is to you and how you've got lots of practice changing diapers for all your nephews and nieces. Just remember to transmit this information with humor, not neediness. You could also try using an introduction service, letting the matchmaker know you want to meet women who are ready to start a family.

Sal, relax and enjoy yourself. Forget about the family thing for a while, and life will probably surprise you when you least expect it.

More Advice

Have a Question?

Do you have a question about how to bring lasting love into your life, determine what you really want in someone, or become an educated consumer of dating resources?

Then please send an e-mail letter to me, at askphilippa@meant2be.com. Please include your first name, city, and state—your privacy will be protected. I can't give personal replies, but I will try to address your concerns in future columns.

Want More?

Read new *"AskPhilippa"* letters and responses each month on the Internet at:

http://www.meant2be.com/Advice.htm/

or simply go to:

meant2be.com

Additional Resources
Meant2Be Products and Services

Additional Resources
Meant2Be Products and Services

Experience the Power of the Meant2Be Personal Learning System

Now that you have read this book, you can imagine having someone in your life who excepts and likes you just the way you are, someone with whom you have all the sizzle, plus the easy-to-be-with comfort of a good friend.

Stop just waiting and wishing and start making it all come true. Achieve results quickly and effectively by ordering and using the complete set of business-practical and heart-centered resources from Meant2Be Unlimited.

Meant2Be Personal Seminar
4 Steps to bring the Right Person into your life Right Now!
– with Philippa Courtney

Only $59.95

Listen, laugh, and learn how to apply sound leadership and achievement principles to your search for love. Philippa Courtney, respected author, speaker, advice columnist, and former Fortune 500 business consultant, shares a business-practical, heart-centered, four-step process that will help you define and meet the right man or woman for you. Enjoy the spontaneity of a live audience, as Philippa recounts her humorous *desperate dating* adventures and as she and her husband candidly answer audience questions about dating, the Meant2Be Process and their relationship. Three 60-minute audiocassettes (90-minute seminar).

Learn to:

– Define the kind of person with whom you can be happiest.
– Combine a logical and intuitive approach to recognizing your right one.
– Deal effectively with heart and hormones.
– Be market smart in how you meet prospective dates.

Meant2Be GuideBook

Only $12.95

A comprehensive learning tool that contains over fifty pages of key points and tips on how to effectively apply the proven Meant2Be Process.

Complete with worksheets and space for note taking, this 8 ½ x 11" book is an indispensable companion to your *Meant2Be Personal Seminar* on audiocassette.

Meant2Be Profile

Only $9.95

A powerful tool designed to help you distinguish your right person from the wrong ones. Takes you through 10 key areas of your life to help you identify the kinds of people with whom you can be happiest. This unique process shows you how to go beyond your analytical thinking and use the power of your unconscious to turn a wish list into the real thing.

Easy to use 8 ½ x 11" format with examples and ample space to write.

Part-1 Identify the traits in others that allow you to feel happy.

Part-2 Define the characteristics, values, goals and styles of your ideal person.

Part-3 Create an EMOTIONAL-SNAPSHOT™ of how you will feel with the right person.

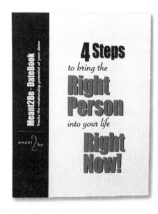

Meant2Be DateBook

Only $9.95

An innovative and practical tool designed to help you quickly and effectively find the right person for you.

An 8 ½ x 11" diary format with charts that help you objectively compare impressions as you date different people. Reinforces the positive by focusing on dates with people you want to see again.

Discover how to:

• Distinguish between lust, romance, and long-term potential.

• Become more aware of how you feel with each person you meet and how feelings change as you get to know each other.

• Clearly understand what you are getting out of relationships, what you are willing to give, and what you ultimately want.

The Complete Meant2Be Package

Only $69.95 – a 25% savings Includes:

- Meant2Be Personal Seminar (on audiocassette)
- Meant2Be GuideBook
- Meant2Be Profile
- Meant2Be DateBook
- Plus three *special bonus* items (not sold separately)
  – How to Write an Effective Romance Ad: expert tips and examples
  – The Meant2Be Dating Resource Evaluator: chart your dating options
  – The Meant2Be Reminder Card - a pocket size affirmation and reminder card

The Meant2Be Tool Kit

Only $29.95 – a 10% savings Includes:

- Meant2Be GuideBook
- Meant2Be Profile
- Meant2Be DateBook

- Plus three *special bonus* items (not sold separately)
  – How to Write an Effective Romance Ad: expert tips and examples
  – The Meant2Be Dating Resource Evaluator: chart your dating options
  – The Meant2Be Reminder Card - a pocket size affirmation and reminder card

Meant2Be Product Order Form

To order: call toll free **1-877-MEANT2Be** (1-877-632-6822)
online at **meant2be.com**
e-mail to **order@meant2be.com**

Qty	Item No.	Title	Price	Amount
	M2B01CP	Complete Meant2Be Package	$69.95	
	M2B01TK	The Meant2Be Tool Kit	$29.95	
	M2B01BK	This Book "4 Steps…"	$14.95	
	M2B01PS	Meant2Be Personal Seminar	$59.95	
	M2B01GB	Meant2Be GuideBook	$12.95	
	M2B01PR	Meant2Be Profile	$9.95	
	M2B01DB	Meant2Be DateBook	$9.95	

	Subtotal	
In California, add sales tax	California Sales Tax	
$3.95 shipping plus $1.00 handling for each item	Shipping & Handling	
$4.95 additional for 2nd day delivery service	Express Delivery	
US only – for international delivery please call	**TOTAL**	

Credit Card

Type: ❑ Visa ❑ MasterCard ❑ American Express ❑ Discover

Number: _____ Exp. Date: ___ / ___

Signature: _____

Your Name: _____

Phone: (____) _____

e-mail: _____

Deliver To:

Name: _____

Address: _____

City: _____

State: _____ Zip Code: _____